Advanced Funk Drumming
A Progressive Approach To Modern Drumset Grooves

- 2nd Edition -

by Jim Payne

Cover design: Scott Bienstock

Interior design and layout: Gerald Vitale

Music engraving: Michael Dawson

Logo design: Trisia Tomanelli

Cover photo: Paul La Raia

Copyright © 2016 by Jim Payne.

All rights reserved. No part of this book or associated media may be reproduced in any form or by any electronic or mechanical means, including information storage and retrieval systems, without permission in writing from the publisher.

International Copyright Secured
Published by Face The Music Productions
P.O.Box 75 Carmel Valley, CA 93924

www.funkydrummer.com

Mac, iPod, and QuickTime are trademarks of Apple Inc., registered in the U.S. and other countries.

TABLE OF CONTENTS

Introduction 4

Acknowledgements 5

Training Videos Online 6

Section 1 – Hi-Hat Openings 8

Section 2 – Ghost Notes 10

Section 3 – 16th-Note Bass Drum Patterns 12

Section 4 – Displace The Backbeat 15

Section 5 – Displaced Backbeats With Ghost Notes 17

Section 6 – More Ghost Notes With 16ths On The Bass Drum 18

Section 7 – Hi-Hat Patterns 20

Section 8 – Paradiddle Possibilities 24

Section 9 – More Hi-Hat Openings 28

Section 10 – Linear Style 30

Section 11 – The Buzz 32

Section 12 – More Ghost Notes 34

Section 13 – Swing Feel 36

Section 14 – Latin Funk 38

Section 15 – Quarter-Note Hi-Hat Accents, Linear Style 46

Section 16 – No "1," Broken Hi-Hat Patterns, Swing Funk 51

Section 17 – Triplet Grooves, Shuffles, Single-Stroke Fill-Ins 54

Section 18 – No "1," Groupings Of Three 16th Notes, Long Buzz 57

Section 19 – Playing Over The "1," On The "1," Four-Bar Phrases 61

Section 20 – Soft Dynamics, Grooves With Pickups,
Long Hi-Hat Openings 64

Section 21 – More Hi-Hat Openings,
Eight-Bar Groove, Use Of 32nd Notes 66

INTRODUCTION

The Beginnings
This project came about when I discovered that I could make surprisingly good videos with my MacBook G3 and a decent external stereo mic. At first I was only going to record some original grooves for my own enjoyment, but then it developed into a more organized and complete project. I had yet to do a follow-up to my *Funk Drumming* book/CD, and now that it was fairly easy for me to record video along with audio, I felt the time was right.

I was in southern France for the summer and had access to a small stone house called a *bergerie* or *cabanon*, on the side of a mountain, where a shepherd might stay for a while to get out of the rain, far away from the main farmhouse…in other words, the perfect place for a drummer! No neighbors above, no neighbors below, no neighbors anywhere nearby. The first video clip and the photos throughout the book give an idea of the location.

There was no electricity, but I didn't need it. If I was careful, the computer's battery had plenty of power for each day's work.

The Concept
Students want to learn how to play various grooves. Some can read, some can't, and some aren't interested. I felt the most helpful instruction would simply be to play the grooves and let you watch and listen to them.

With this in mind I recorded these video clips and put them in loop format so that you can play along with them until you master them. Transcriptions are available in the book for those who want to follow them and see what it all looks like. The book text also includes some tips on individual beats.

I did not spend a lot of time on methodical exercises to develop each of the techniques (ghost notes, accents, bass drum doubles, etc), but I've included one or two beats for each technique. My book *Funk Drumming* deals with some of these techniques in a more detailed and methodical fashion. If you find, for example, that your left-hand doubles aren't cutting it, you'll have to practice them independently. Likewise with the 16th-note doubles on the bass drum and the constant 16ths on the hi-hat. (The down/up technique is best understood by watching the video clips.)

If one particular beat is just too difficult—for instance, a beat with three left-hand ghost notes in a row—skip over that beat and go on to the first rhythms in the next section. It's more important to understand the general concepts in each section than it is to be able to play the most difficult beats.

Slow And Fast
I was very concerned about being able to slow down the tempo for the purpose of understanding the rhythms. It seems that everyone tries to play everything up to speed the first time around, and even though we think it's somehow going to work, it usually doesn't. The brain has to really understand what to do, before it can execute the ideas at full speed.

With this in mind I recorded many of the beats in two versions, A and B. A is slower and B is faster. There is only one transcription, because both versions look alike, but there are two video clips, two iPod videos, and two MP3 files.

Organization
As far as the organization goes, the first half, Sections 1 through 14, is set up in a progressive manner; simpler techniques are included first, and then we move on to more complicated grooves, although some of these sections also have some advanced beats.

Everyone is at a different playing level, so there's nothing wrong with sampling some of the beats in any section. If they interest you, work on those for a while, or jump around from section to section.

Each of Sections 15 through 21 represents a day's work. There is no real organization, and I'm really playing off the top of my head. Different techniques are used and explained in the text, but each section contains the grooves I came up with on that particular day.

Of course, the beats are just the beginning. I expect you to take these ideas and develop them further to create the next generation of funk.

Good luck, and all the best,

Jim Payne

www.funkydrummer.com

ACKNOWLEDGEMENTS

Jim's Note
I'd like to acknowledge my debt of gratitude to my drumming and musical inspirations and musical partners.

Drummers
Billy Deare, Jabo Starks, Clyde Stubblefield, Nate Jones, Woody Woodson, Elvin Jones, Dannie Richmond, Mike Clark, Max Roach, Tito Puente, Orestes Vilato, Jamey Haddad, Tony Williams, Lenny White, Joe Morello, Jeff Williams, Jim Strassburg, Roger Hawkins, Roger Humphries, Jeff "Tain" Watts, Eddie Locke, Clayton Fillyau, David Garibaldi, Bernard Purdie, Philly Joe Jones, Jimmy Madison, Billy Hart, Joe Dukes, Sonny Freeman, Ray Lucas, and Roy McCurdy.

Musicians/Artists
John Coltrane, Michael Brecker, O.V. Wright, B.B. King, Joe Tex, Herbie Hancock, Joe Henderson, Steve Cropper, Larry Young, Joe Farrell, James Moody, Linc Chamberlain, Otis Redding, Freddie King, Dave Liebman, Billy Stewart, Thelonious Monk, Walter Davis, Jr., Horace Silver, Vincent van Gogh, James Brown, and the rhythm section who played on Jimmy Reed's hits, whoever they were.

Musical Partners
Fred Wesley, Pee Wee Ellis, Maceo Parker, John Scofield, Mark Helias, Al Jaffe, Ray Anderson, Steve Elson, Mike Clark, Oz Noy, Bob Greenlee, Lucky Peterson, Ace Moreland, Kermit Young, Frank Palmer, Burt Shurly, Ben Stivers, Jerry Z., Al Street, Adam Klipple, Evan Palmerston, Bill Bickford, Marc Puricelli, Eric Person, and Gene Torres.

Dedication
To my loving wife of twenty-nine years, Joanna FitzPatrick. I definitely couldn't do it without you, chérie.
To my children, Sam and Amie, you're the best.
And to my brother, Giles, and his wife, Lucia. Thanks for your support.

Special Thanks
Bill Miller (1961–2008), Mike Dawson, Gerald Vitale, Tracy Kearns, Scott Bienstock, Isabel Spagnardi, Trisia Tomanelli, Bill Bay, Jill Newman, Philippe and Carole de Ville, Carlton Bright, Michael Lydon, and Pres. Daisaku Ikeda of SGI, www.sgi-usa.com.

Endorsements
Jim Payne endorses **Paiste** cymbals, **Ludwig** drums, **Vater** sticks, and **Remo** drumheads.

HOW TO DOWNLOAD THE ACCOMPANYING VIDEO FILES

After you purchase Advanced Funk Drumming via the website www.funkydrummer.com you will receive a link in the e-mail that was used for your purchase. Click this link to download all the video files.

These files are quite large so it will take some time to download them.

Please check your SPAM folder if you do not receive the link in your INBOX.

If you're still having trouble accessing the videos, please submit a request in the CONTACT section of www.funkydrummer.com

NOTATION KEY

NOTATION KEY

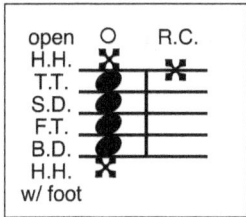

Open Hi-Hat Notation

1. An "o" over a hi-hat note means to strike the hi-hat while it's open. It is assumed that the left foot will close the hi-hat at the end of that note. In the following example the snare drum is also played when the hi-hat is closed on beat 4.

2. When you need to play notes on other parts of the kit while the hi-hat is open, a tie will be used from the opening of the hi-hat until the closing. Any notes under this tie will be played while the hi-hat is open. The left foot closes the hi-hat at the "+" sign.

In the following example, the "+" sign on beat 1 of the first bar does not affect the first bar of the beat, but when the beat is repeated, it indicates that the hi-hat is closed with the left foot on beat 1. In this case the bass drum is also played on "1" when the beat is repeated.

3. Another way to indicate a hi-hat closing is by adding an "x" below the staff at the closing point. This indicates that the left foot will close the hi-hat at this point. In the following example the hi-hat is closed on the "e" of beat 1.

SECTION 1
Hi-Hat Openings

Hi-hat openings are a distinctive characteristic of funk. They can be used to add some spice and variation to the rhythm, particularly in the second measure of a two-measure phrase.

The open hi-hat is indicated by an "o" above the hi-hat note. The general rule is that the hi-hat stays open for the value of the note below the "o." It's understood that the left foot will then close the hi-hat at the beginning of the next note.

1.01 In this rhythm the hi-hat is opened on the **"& of 3."** The "& of 3" is the "&" **after** "3." Likewise, the **"& of 1"** is the "&" **after** "1," and so on. This is common drummer and musician talk used to pinpoint a particular spot in a measure.

In this beat the hi-hat is opened on the **"& of 3"** and closed with the left foot on "4." The left hand also plays the snare drum on "4" while the right hand plays the closed hi-hat. The right hand, left hand, and left foot all come down on 4. (Left-handed drummers should reverse these stickings.)

1.02 Here the hi-hat is opened on the "& of 4" and then closed on "1" of the next measure when the beat is repeated. The bass drum is also played on "1." The right hand, right foot, and left foot all come down on "1" when the beat is repeated.

1.03 The hi-hat is opened and played along with the bass drum on the "& of 3." The right hand, left hand, and left foot come down on "4."

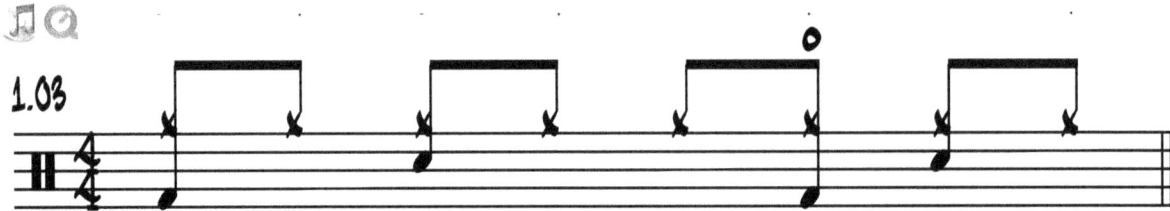

ADVANCED FUNK DRUMMING

1.04 Similar to 1.03, with added bass drum notes.

SECTION 2

Ghost Notes

Ghost notes are used throughout funk drumming to create a rolling 16th-note pulse underneath the groove. The key here (and this is very, *very* important!) is that the ghost notes are played much softer than the backbeats, or accented snare drum notes. **David Garibaldi** suggests that the stick should start one inch or less above the snare drum for ghost notes. Check the QuickTime video examples.

Ghost notes should be only as loud as normal hi-hat notes played with the tip of the stick.

The louder snare drum notes (the backbeats on 2 and 4) now have **accents** (>) underneath to distinguish them from the much softer ghost notes. These accented snare drum notes can simply be louder notes on the snare drum or rimshots.

Rimshots

Rimshots are made by hitting the snare drum head and the snare drum rim at the same time. This produces a sharp "crack" sound. As **Tito Puente** once said to me when referring to a timbale rimshot, "Beautiful sound, isn't it? Beautiful!"

The sound of rimshots will vary depending on how much of the stick you use between the rim of the snare drum and the tip of the stick. More stick will give a fatter sound. When the stick is closer to the rim, you'll get a more high-pitched, timbale-like sound. Also, rimshots, like normal snare drum notes, can be louder or softer depending on how much force you use.

16th-Note Count

Notice the 16th-note count written above the rhythms: **1 e & a 2 e & a 3 e & a 4 e & a.**
(The "a" is pronounced "ah.")

It's important to become very familiar with this count because most of the notes in funk will be played on these counts. The 16th-note count should also make it easier to read the notation because all the notes will be lined up beneath the corresponding numbers, letters, and &s of the count.

I recommend singing the count in your head (or out loud if you're not worried about people thinking you're a little crazy!) as you walk or drive from place to place. When you get very familiar with this count, you will be able to take your mind off it slightly while working on a beat, but the count should still be going in your head. Then you can refer to it when you need to clarify what's happening at any particular point in the rhythm.

Most of the following beats in Section 2 are classic **James Brown**–type beats. This style was pioneered in the '60s by one of Brown's very influential drummers, **Clayton Fillyau**. He can be heard on *James Brown Live At The Apollo* (1962).

2.04 A&B The two ghost notes on the "&" and "a of 2" can be bounced. If they're not coming out cleanly, you may have to work some more on your double strokes.

SECTION 3

16th-Note Bass Drum Patterns

Slow it down! Sixteenth-note bass drum patterns are one of the quantum leaps that separate funk from rock. An accomplished funk drummer has to have a "good foot." The bass drum really drives the band in funk, much as the ride cymbal drives the band in jazz.

3.01 Not much trouble here because there's only one bass drum 16th note on the **"a of 1."** The "a of 1" is the "a" after "1." Likewise the **"& of 1"** is the "&" after "1," and so on. This is common drummer and musician talk used to pinpoint a particular spot in a measure.

16th-Note Doubles On The Bass Drum

Starting with beat 3.02, the right foot has to play almost twice as many bass drum notes as it does in most rock. The two 16ths in a row on the bass drum are called 16th-note doubles. Playing doubles on the bass drum will require some practice time. Start *very* slowly, use a metronome, and try to relax the leg muscles after each double.

Practice for short periods of time, say 5 to 7 minutes, and no more. Do this as part of your practice routine each day. Longer sessions of playing bass drum doubles could end up straining your bass drum foot and leg muscles, and this may take several days to heal. If you do decide to practice 16th doubles more than once on the same day, spend 15 to 30 minutes practicing something else before starting the doubles a second time.

Slow, steady practice develops speed. One of my teachers, **Sonny Igoe**, always said, **"Practice slow to play fast."** Of course, he followed his own advice, and, believe me, he was amazingly fast!

If you're practicing too fast, playing sloppily without the proper space between the notes, playing at the very edge of your ability, and making mistakes, you're wasting your time. You're practicing making mistakes! You might as well be watching TV.

At first, the slower the better for the 16th-note doubles. You've just got to put some time into this. There's no other way. Practice 3.02 for a couple of days using the above practice method, then go on.

I would spend at least a week on 3.02, 3.03, 3.04, 3.05, 3.06, 3.07, and 3.08 before moving on. Take one of these beats each day and play it for 5 to 7 minutes.

These beats can be slowed down using the QuickTime menu at the top of the screen: Window > Show AV Controls > Playback Speed functions. See Introduction.

3.04 A&B This is where the fun really begins. Playing on an "a" followed by a number on the bass drum is not easy. Follow the above instructions, and, like anything else, if you work at it you'll get it. And use reason. Don't try to learn it in one day by practicing 8 hours straight. Believe me, that won't work.

3.07

1 E & A 2 E & A 3 E & A 4 E & A 1 E & A 2 E & A 3 E & A 4 E & A

3.08

1 E & A 2 E & A 3 E & A 4 E & A 1 E & A 2 E & A 3 E & A 4 E & A

3.09

1 E & A 2 E & A 3 E & A 4 E & A 1 E & A 2 E & A 3 E & A 4 E & A

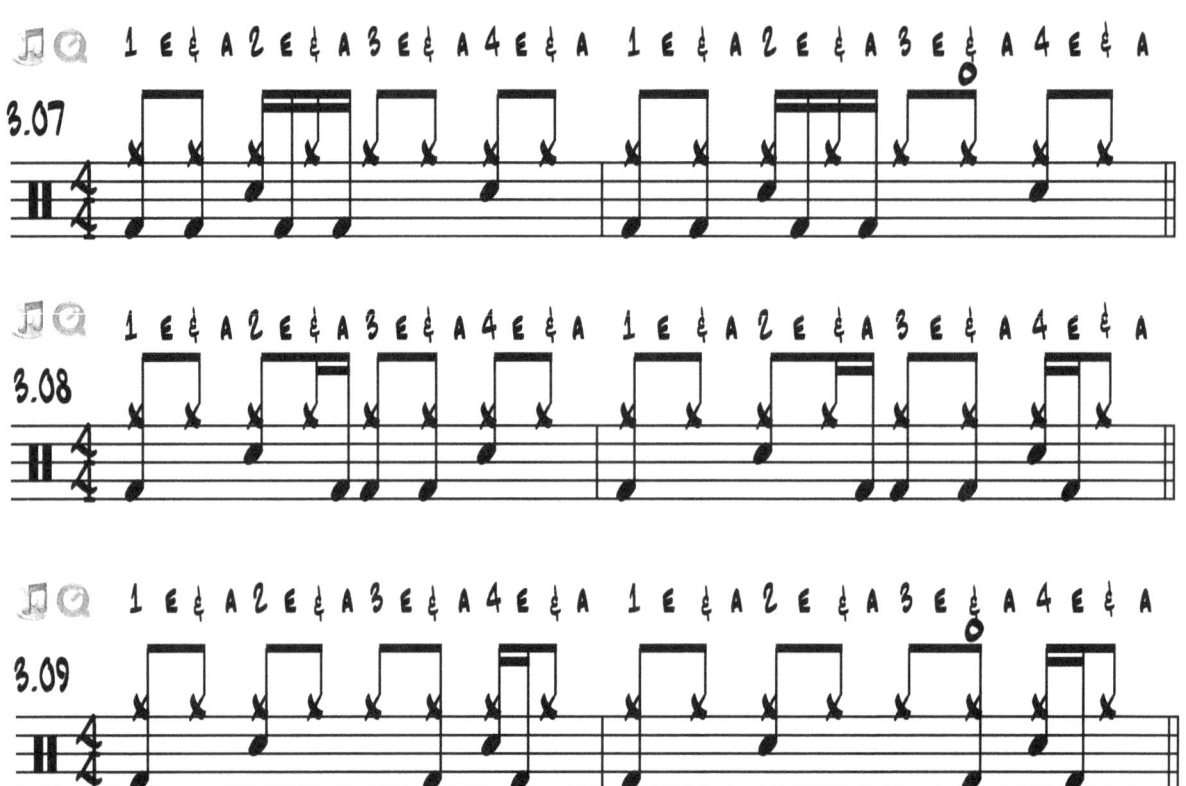

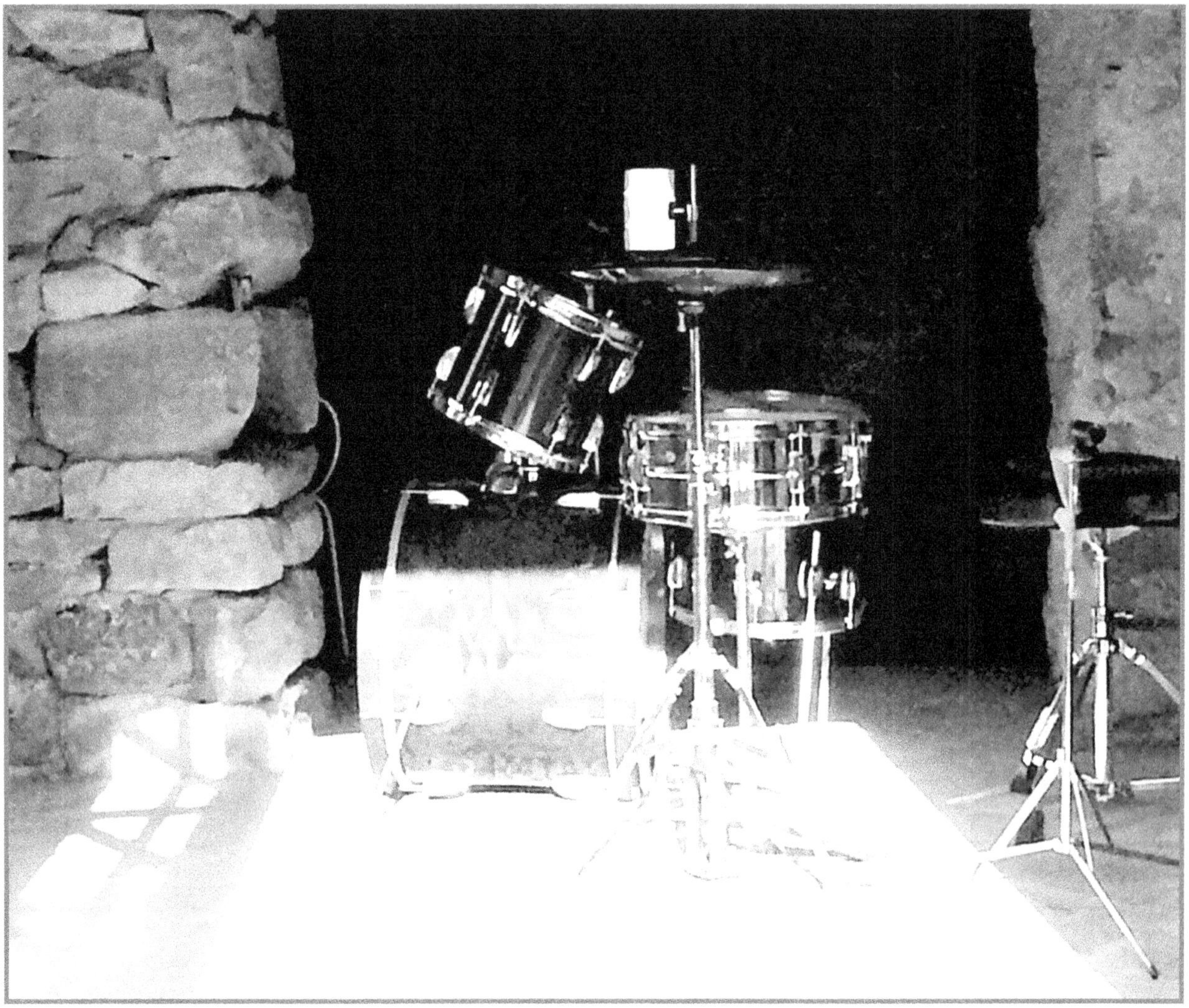

SECTION 4

Displace The Backbeat

The first time I heard a dispaced backbeat was on **James Brown's** 1963 album *Pure Dynamite!/Live At The Royal* with **Clayton Fillyau** on drums. **Clyde Stubblefield**, another JB drummer, incorporated this concept into JB's famous **"Cold Sweat"** (1967), a song that became a very influential classic. We're so used to hearing and feeling the backbeat on 2 and 4 that displacing it to another part of the beat really shakes up the rhythm in an exciting way.

The snare drum can be played normally or with a rimshot on these beats.

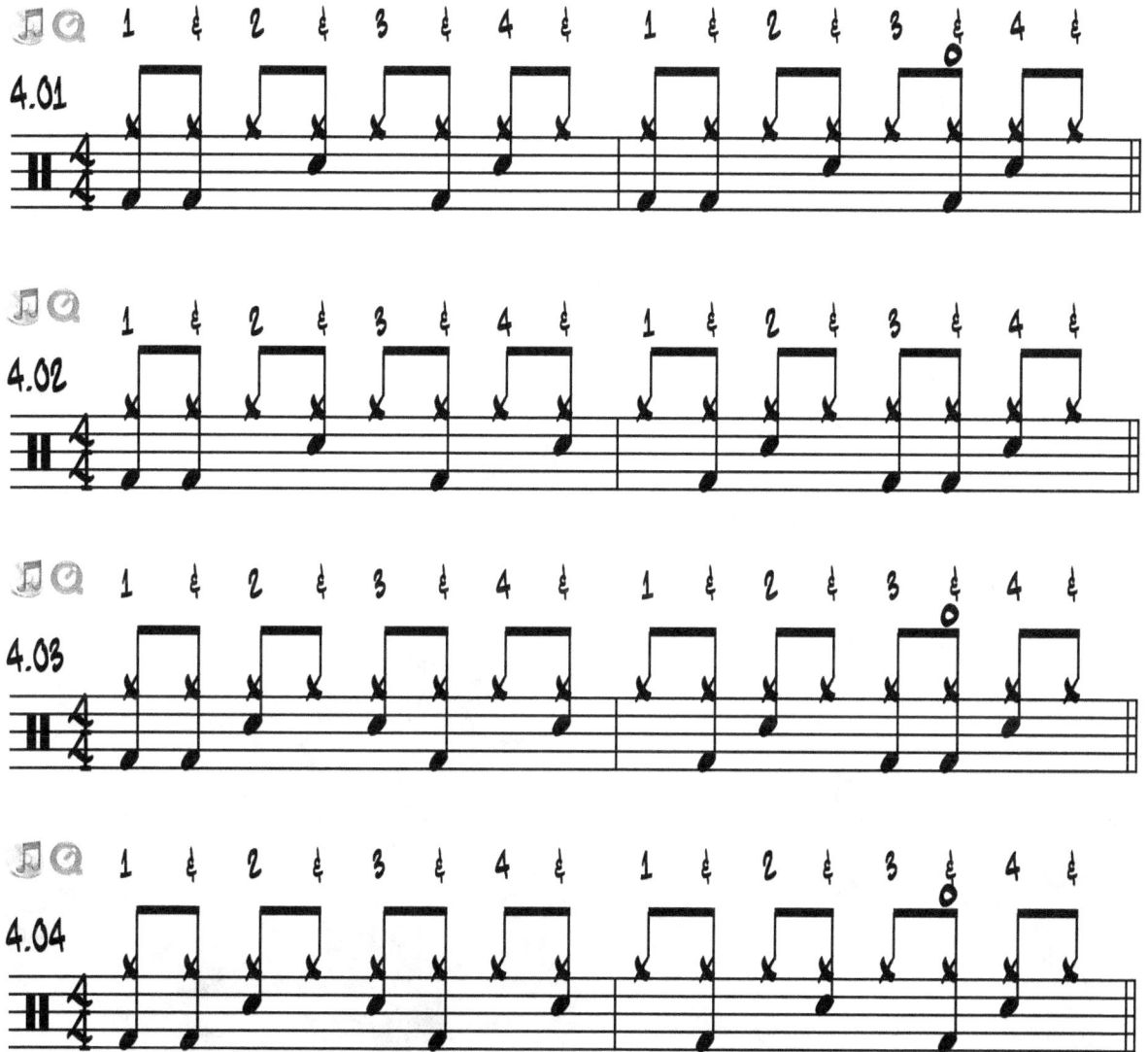

4.05 Harvey Mason was the first drummer I heard play a snare drum accent on the "a of 1." It's really an orchestration of the 3-2 Afro-Cuban son clave spread around the drumset. Harvey used this displacement on **Herbie Hancock's "Chameleon"** (1973). All snare drum notes should be played with equal volume. They can also be played as rimshots.

4.06 This is a signature R&B/funk lick. Playing the "e of 3" and "4" gives the rhythm a kick or jump. I played all snare drum notes as rimshots in the videos. I was playing this lick in a soundcheck when I was with the **JB Horns (Maceo Parker, Pee Wee Ellis, and Fred Wesley)**. Pee Wee said, "Yeah, give me some more of that behind my solos!" Fred said, "Yeah, me too." They liked the syncopation as opposed to the usual backbeats on 2 and 4.

SECTION 5
Displaced Backbeats With Ghost Notes

Adding ghost notes to displaced backbeat grooves can make the rhythm super-funky. Again, play the ghost notes as soft as possible. It doesn't matter if you miss a few times before you get it right. See how soft you can go.

5.01 A&B This is close to **Clyde Stubblefield's** famous **"Cold Sweat"** beat.

5.03 A&B Here's the Harvey Mason accent on the "a of 1" with ghost notes added.

SECTION 6

More Ghost Notes With 16ths On The Bass Drum

Now we'll add ghost notes to the bass drum patterns we've learned so far.

6.01 A&B

6.02 A&B

6.03 A&B These beats containing 16th-note doubles on the "a of 2" and "3" should be played very slowly at first. Make sure the doubles are clear and distinct with the proper space between them. Practicing too fast is a waste of time.

It's also nice to accent the second of the two doubles, in this case the bass drum on "3."

6.03 A&B

6.04 A&B Here's a common skip-type accent on the "e of 3" and on "4" (second measure).

6.04 A&B

ADVANCED FUNK DRUMMING

SECTION 7
Hi-Hat Patterns

This section covers some of the most popular hi-hat patterns in funk. There are endless variations of snare and bass drum patterns to combine with these hi-hat patterns. If you can master the following examples, you will get a good idea of which patterns you want to study further.

My book **Funk Drumming** deals with this concept in a more thorough and methodical way (see pages 39–41). Superimpose the various hi-hat patterns over these beats. Extensive ghost-note exercises with various hi-hat patterns are on pages 78–83.

7.01 A&B This hi-hat pattern was used by **Jabo Starks** on **James Brown's "Soul Power"** (1971).

Swing Feel In Funk

Whenever you have two 16ths in a row on the hi-hat or bass drum, as in 7.01 and the following rhythms, you can put a little swing into it by shuffling those two notes, i.e., playing them more like 16th-note triplets with a 16th note–triplet rest in between. The subtle variations between straight 16ths and 16th-note triplets are not something that can be written out.

You can actually put this shuffle feel on any notes that fall on "e" or "a," whether they're on the snare, bass drum, hi-hat, or cymbal.

If you listen to Jabo's playing on "Soul Power," you'll hear how this works. He was a jazz/R&B drummer before he joined James Brown, and he put some swing feel into his rhythms. You can experiment and try putting a lot or a little swing into it. This feel is something that you can just fall into without thinking too much about it.

7.02 A&B Hi-hat pattern of one 8th and two 16ths throughout. This pattern can be easily shaded toward the jazz ride pattern. All of your jazz independence can then be applied to funk as well!

ADVANCED FUNK DRUMMING

7.04 A&B The standard 16th-note funk hi-hat pattern.

The tempo must be fairly slow in order to play this beat because the right hand has to play a lot of notes in succession.

Check the video for the **down/up motion** of the right hand, wrist and forearm. You can catch the hi-hat on the "up" stroke for every second note. On the downstroke, play the shank of the stick (the fat part below the tip) on the edge of the hi-hat, and on the upstroke, bring up the wrist and tap the top of the hi-hat with the tip of the stick.

Squeeze the fulcrum (where you hold the stick, between the first and second joints of the forefinger and the fleshy part of the thumb) on the way down for the first 16th note, and then relax the fulcrum and strike the second 16th as the hand and wrist come back up to get ready for the next pair.

This down/up technique will also produce an accent on the first of every two notes, which can add more drive to the rhythm.

7.05 A&B Accents on the first of every two 16th notes can also be added, as in 7.04.

7.07 A&B This quarter-note hi-hat style is derived from the Latin cha-cha cowbell pattern.

Since we're so used to playing continual 8th notes on the hi-hat, this beat will take some practice. For some reason, it's a little more difficult when the four limbs have to play individually on parts of a rhythm. For example, I've always found it's easier to play the right hand and the right foot together than it is to play the right foot by itself.

Clyde Stubblefield popularized this style on **James Brown's "Say It Loud – I'm Black And I'm Proud"** (1968) and **"Mother Popcorn (Part 1)"** (1969), and also on **Pee Wee Ellis's "In The Middle (Part 1)"** (1968). All these beats are transcribed in my book *100 Famous Funk Beats*.

7.09 A&B This offbeat hi-hat style became popular when **Eric Clapton,** with drummer **Jamie Oldaker,** had a big hit with his cover of **Bob Marley's** reggae song **"I Shot The Sheriff"** (1974). Accenting the hi-hat on the "&" implies a **double-time feel**, which can really help move the rhythm along.

This is not easy to do, but it can be mastered, like anything else, with a little practice. By adding an accent on the hi-hat, you've added another layer of sound. You have to get used to hearing this. The process of making music is not so much reading notes off a piece of paper and translating that information to your limbs as it is hearing the sounds in your head and then playing them with your hands and feet. Once you get used to hearing this feel, it will become easier.

In this case we are adding a fourth sound, the accented hi-hat, along with the unaccented hi-hat, the bass drum, and the snare. Spend some time with Example 7.09 until you can play and hear a real difference between the accented and unaccented hi-hat notes. You can use the down/up technique described for 7.04, only this time in reverse. Use the tip of the stick on top of the hi-hat for the downbeats and the shank of the stick on the side of the hi-hat for each "&."

This right-hand pattern can also be used on the ride cymbal. To do that, play the downbeats with the tip of the stick just below the bell of the cymbal and each "&" with the shank of the stick on the bell. Then add the hi-hat with the left foot on quarter notes, on 2 and 4, or on every "&."

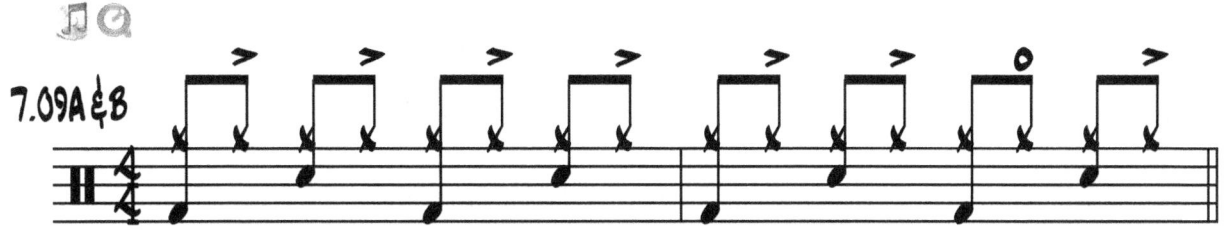

7.11 Here's the same kind of feel but using a slightly different technique. The hi-hat is played only on each "&." This pattern also works well with the right hand playing the bell of the ride cymbal on "&" with the shank of the stick.

7.12 This is almost a linear pattern. (More on this concept later.) In this beat, the "& of 3" is the only place where two limbs are playing together. The right hand can also play the bell of the ride.

SECTION 8
Paradiddle Possibilities

8.01 These beats involve playing a paradiddle between the hi-hat and snare drum. When the single paradiddle sticking (RLRR, LRLL) is played with the right hand on the hi-hat and left hand on the snare drum, the left hand falls naturally on the snare drum on 2 and 4, which can then be easily accented for the backbeats, either as a rimshot or a louder snare drum note.

Play these beats without the hi-hat accents at first, and then add them. The accents add another layer of sound, as in each accented "&" of 7.09. This may be difficult to incorporate at first, but it's well worth the effort because the accents make the rhythms much more interesting, and much more funky!

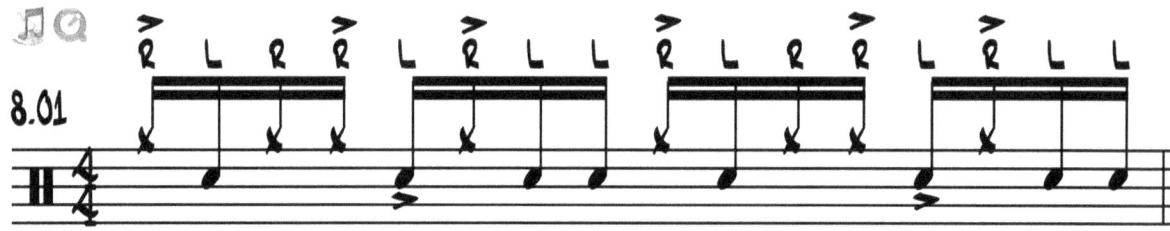

8.02 Add the bass drum.

8.03 Another bass drum pattern.

8.04 The King Kong Rhythm.

David Garibaldi learned this rhythm from **Pete DePoe**, who played with the band **Redbone**. Pete used it on a song called **"The Prehistoric Rhythm With The King Kong Beat."** David used it on the amazingly funky **"Soul Vaccination"** (1973) with **Tower Of Power**. The hi-hat accents outline the three side of the 3-2 Afro-Cuban son clave.

8.05 Add the bass drum.

8.06 Another bass drum pattern.

A club somewhere

Another club, somewhere else

Sound check at the 2006 PASIC Percussion Convention. Austin, Texas.

Blue Note, NYC.

SECTION 9

More Hi-Hat Openings

9.01 A&B The hi-hat is opened on the "a of 1" and closed with the left foot on "2." The snare drum is also played on "2." The right hand doesn't need to play the hi-hat on "2" because the snare accent covers up the hi-hat sound anyway. Also, it's a lot easier to play this way.

Ringo Starr was the first drummer I saw who didn't always play the closed hi-hat with the right hand along with the backbeat on the snare drum.

9.02 A&B The open hi-hat played on "4" stays open until "1" of the next bar, when the beat is repeated. This closing is indicated with an "x" for the left foot in the lower part of the staff, just below the bass drum.

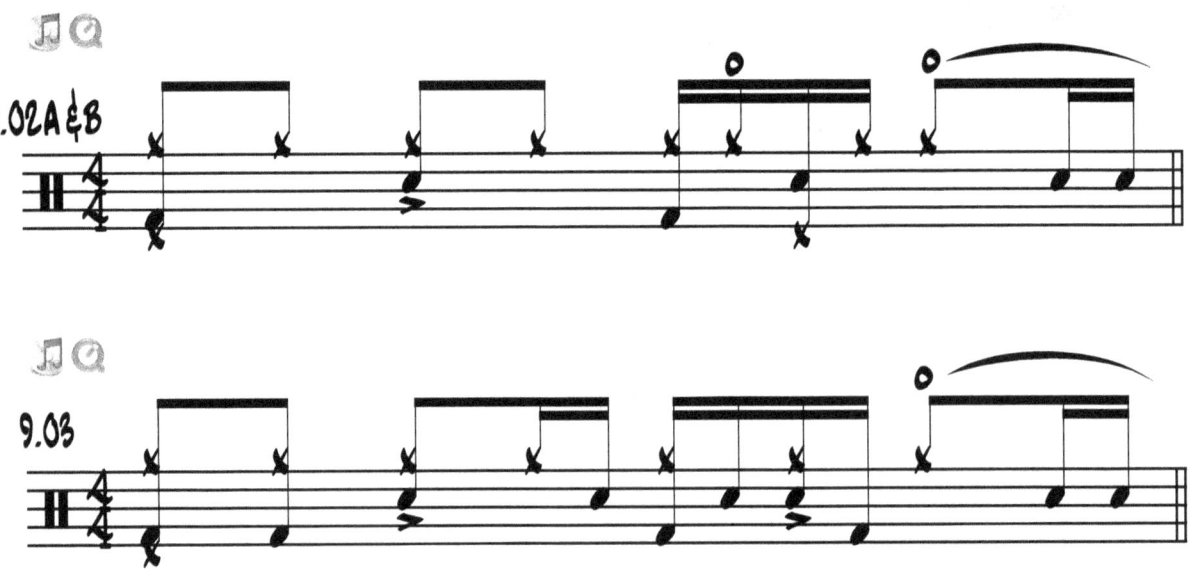

9.04 This groove incorporates the King Kong hi-hat pattern into the second half of the measure.

9.05 This beat has a quarter-note hi-hat opening on "1." The hi-hat stays open until "2."

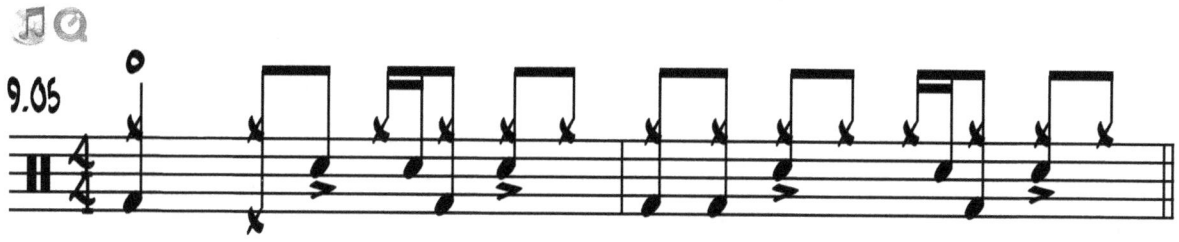

9.06 A&B Now the quarter notes are accented.

9.07 A&B This rhythm has **Bernard Purdie's** signature hi-hat/bass drum lick that he used on **Aretha Franklin's "Rock Steady"** (1971).

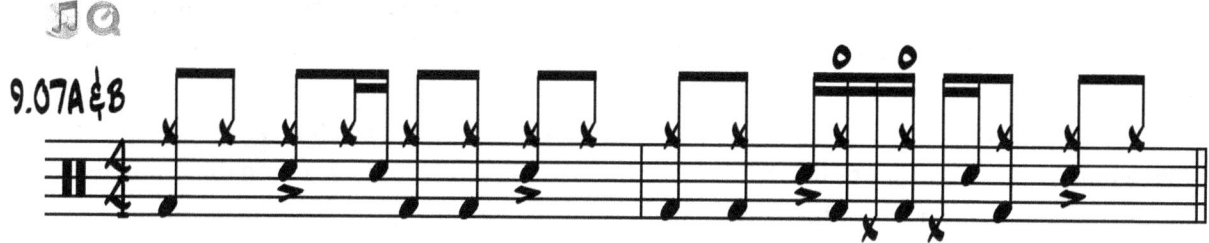

9.08 This beat incorporates a more unusual hi-hat opening. The snare drum is played along with the opening.

9.09 A&B In this rhythm, the hi-hat is opened on "1" and is immediately closed on the "a of 1."

SECTION 10

Linear Style

Rock and funk drummers often play a constant stream of 8th notes on the hi-hat. Bass and snare drum patterns are usually thought of as being played against or underneath these 8th notes on the hi-hat. As funk developed into a constant flow of 16th notes, drummers realized that they didn't have to play everything against a steady 8th-note hi-hat pattern.

It was a change in the way rhythms were heard. Instead of hearing one rhythm against another, drummers started hearing a flow of 16th notes, **one at a time**, on various pieces of the kit (usually on the bass drum, snare drum, and hi-hat). This opened up a lot of new possibilities and actually made it easier to play more complex rhythms.

Also, rudimental snare drum technique spread **between** the hi-hat and snare drum could be used to produce the 16th-note flow drummers were looking for. When the bass drum was added to these rudimental stickings as a third voice, as explained by **Gary Chaffee** in his *Patterns* books, it became a recipe for some very funky new grooves. **Mike Clark** and **David Garibaldi** pioneered this style.

One more point: The basic linear concept—playing only one sound surface at a time—doesn't mean that you *can't* add elements with two or more sounds playing together. There are no "linear police" checking to make sure only one sound is being played at a time. In fact, most so-called linear beats combine one-part coordination (one limb played at a time) with two- and three-part coordination (two and three limbs played at a time). The entire beat does not have to be linear. See **Dahlgren and Fine's** book *4-Way Coordination* for detailed coordination exercises. I have found these very useful for building funk and jazz coordination chops.

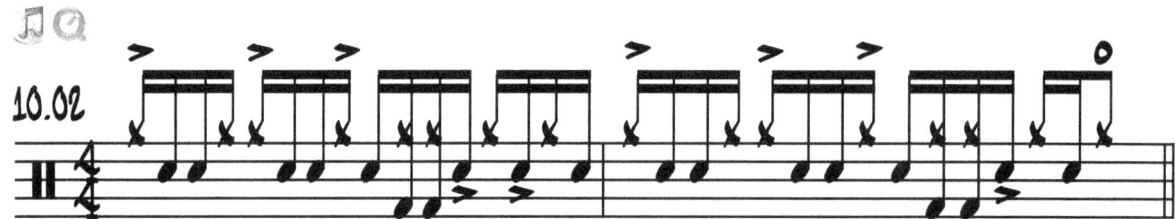

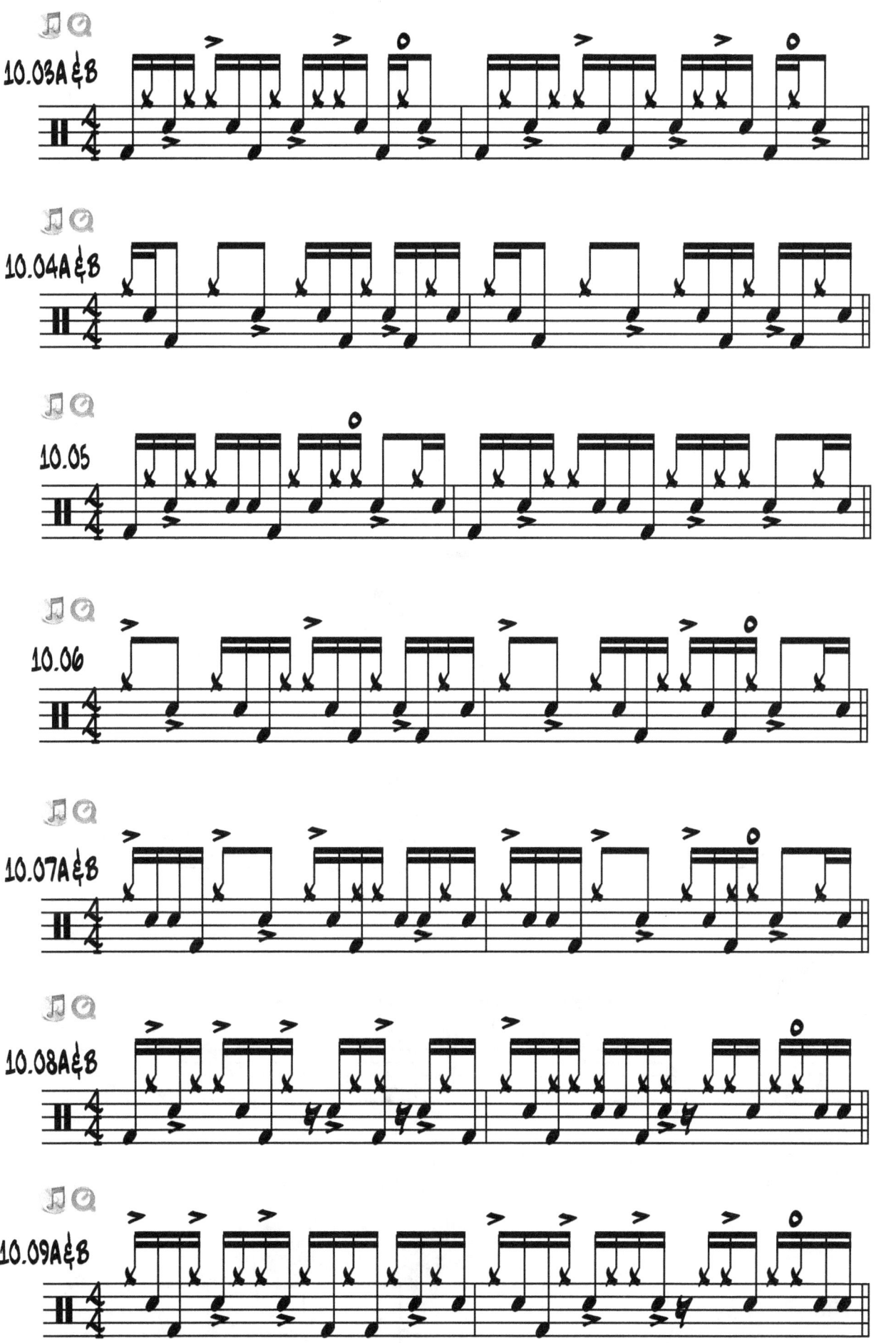

SECTION 11
The Buzz

Buzz strokes are usually played on the 16th note before the downbeat (the first beat of a measure) or the 16th note before any bass drum beat that falls on the quarter notes—1, 2, 3, or 4.

It can be played in two ways:

1. Start on the last 16th note before the bass drum note (the "a") and play a 32nd-note double stroke with the left hand, i.e., two notes in the space of one 16th note.

2. Start on the last 16th note before a bass drum note and simply drag the left stick on the snare drum as a pickup into the bass drum note. This is the same technique that is used in the buzz roll. Check the QuickTime clips.

11.04 A&B In this groove, the buzz is used on the backbeat, "2", to create a softer, less defined sound. Buzzes can be used when you don't want to accent 2 and 4 equally.

SECTION 12

More Ghost Notes

12.01 A&B In this beat, the ghost note on the "& of 1" is played along with the bass drum. This creates a nice variation with a fuller sound.

12.01A&B

12.02A&B

12.03A&B

12.04A&B

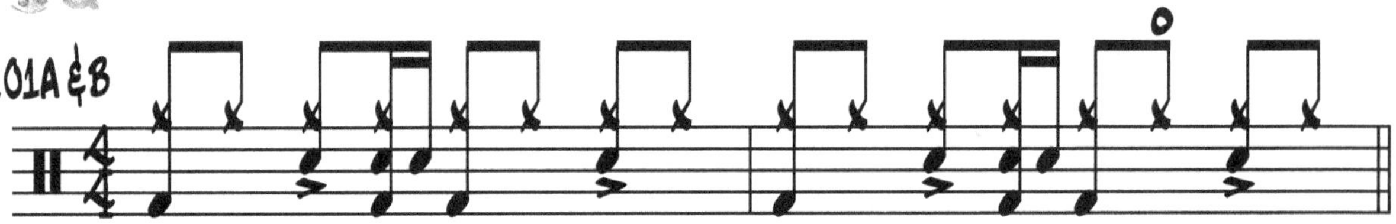

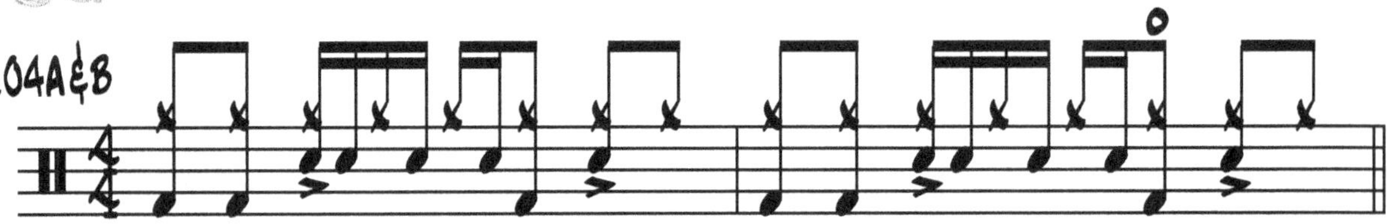

12.05 A&B This style of three left-hand 16ths in a row with the accent on the second one was used by **Clyde Stubblefield**. The more you relax, the easier it is. Clyde loves this and used it on several James Brown songs, including **"I Got The Feelin'"** (1968) and **"Mother Popcorn"** (1969).

12.05A&B

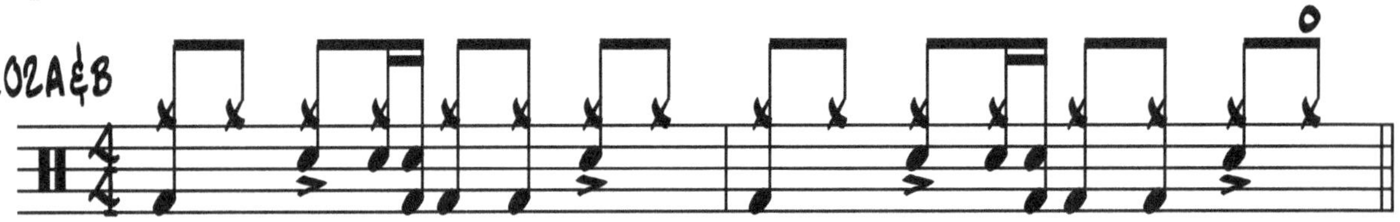

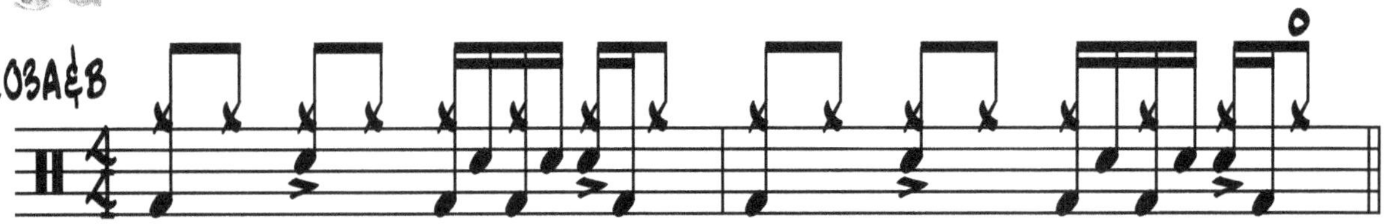

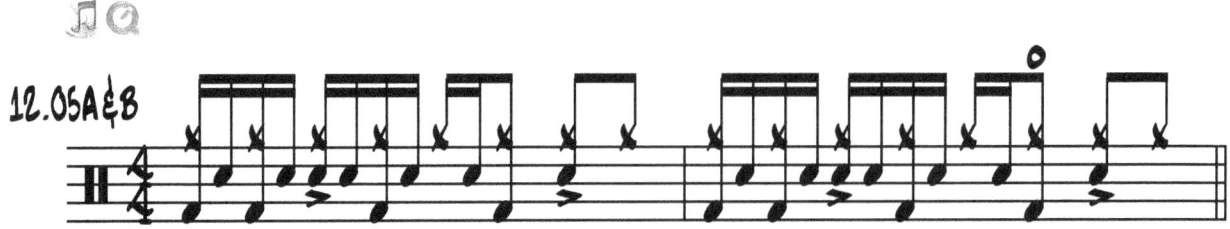

Joanna FitzPatrick

SECTION 13
Swing Feel

Drummers like **Jabo Starks**, who played a lot of jazz grooves and shuffles with **Bobby Bland** before becoming a super funkster with **James Brown**, put some swing feel into the funk. It's a feel that's in-between straight 16ths and 16th-note triplets. It really can't be notated accurately, but it's not hard to understand once you listen to it. You can add different degrees of swing feel to funk, but normally after listening and experimenting a little you'll settle into a feel you like.

13.02 A&B Ghost note with bass drum on the "e of 3."

13.03 A&B Sixteenth-note triplets after "3."

13.04 Ghost note on "4" followed by an accented snare drum note on the "e of 4" (measure 1).

13.06 I added some improvisation the second time through on the movie and audio tracks.

13.08 Ghost notes and bass drum notes together on "e" and the "&" of "3."

SECTION 14
Latin Funk

The basic idea here is to use a Latin cowbell pattern in the right hand and then add the left-hand and bass drum parts. It's important to master the hand pattern before adding the bass drum.

I used to think of funk as a conversation between the snare drum and the bass drum while the right hand played a constant 8th-note pattern on the hi-hat. The main voices I was hearing were the bass drum and snare drum.

When I began incorporating right hand hi-hat variations, I found that hearing the hands first and then adding the bass drum seemed to make more sense. A complicated 16th-note pattern can become easier to play, just by thinking about it in a different way.

3-2 Latin Cascara

14.01 This is the standard 3-2 Latin cascara pattern in 16th-note form.

14.02 Add right hand accents. It's worth it to work on this until you have it down pat. This will make it easier to add other elements later. The accents provide another interesting layer of sound. This pattern can also be used for your traditional Latin drumset repertoire.

14.03 Substitute left hand accents on the snare drum for some of the cascara notes. This is another application of the linear style. You're still playing the same basic cascara rhythm, but now you're orchestrating it between the hi-hat and the snare drum.

14.04 Add the bass drum. The main difference between the Latin concept and the funk concept is that the Latin rhythm section, in which the congas cover the lower range, usually accents "4," whereas in funk "1" is usually accented. That's where the phrase **"on the 1"** comes from—a strong downbeat with the bass drum on the "1" of the measure.

I find the following bass drum pattern always works well in funk. Jabo Starks' beat on James Brown's **"Soul Power"** is a good example. You don't have to play a lot of 16th notes on the bass drum when the hands are playing a more complex pattern.

14.05 A&B This is one of my favorite bass drum patterns. Starting on the "& of 3," it's a grouping of the first of each three 16th notes: the "& of 3," then the "e of 4," then "1."

This pattern has the effect of cycling the bass drum into "1", or falling into "1", because it has a pulse based on three-note groupings.

So we have a combination of a linear hand pattern and bass drum beats that go along with the right hand.

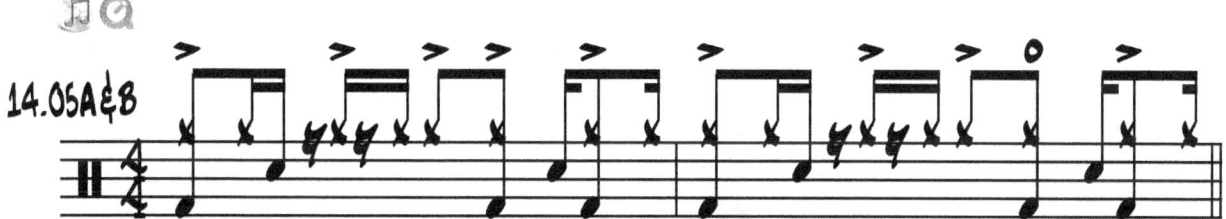

ADVANCED FUNK DRUMMING

Fill-In Style

The next few examples use what I call a fill-in style to create a flow of steady 16th notes. We'll start again with the 3-2 cascara.

14.07 Add right hand accents.

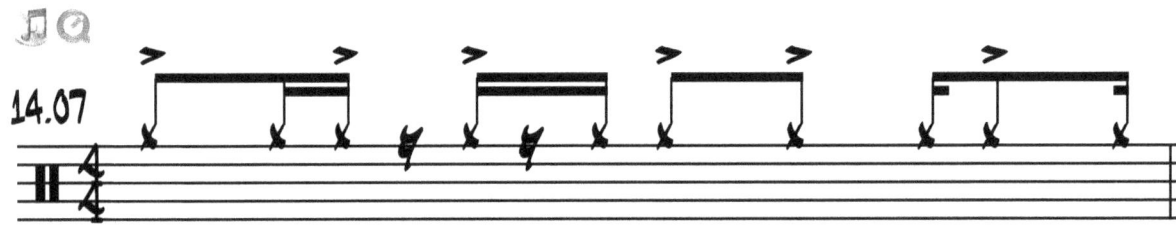

14.08 Fill in all notes not played by the right hand with left hand snare notes. This sounds complicated, but it's not all that difficult if you've studied your rudiments or done any hand-to-hand playing. Play left hand ghost notes on the snare whenever the right hand is not playing the hi-hat.

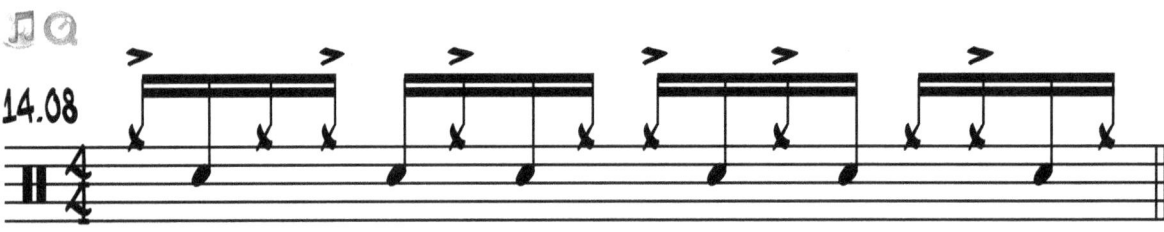

14.09 Choose some snare drum notes to accent.

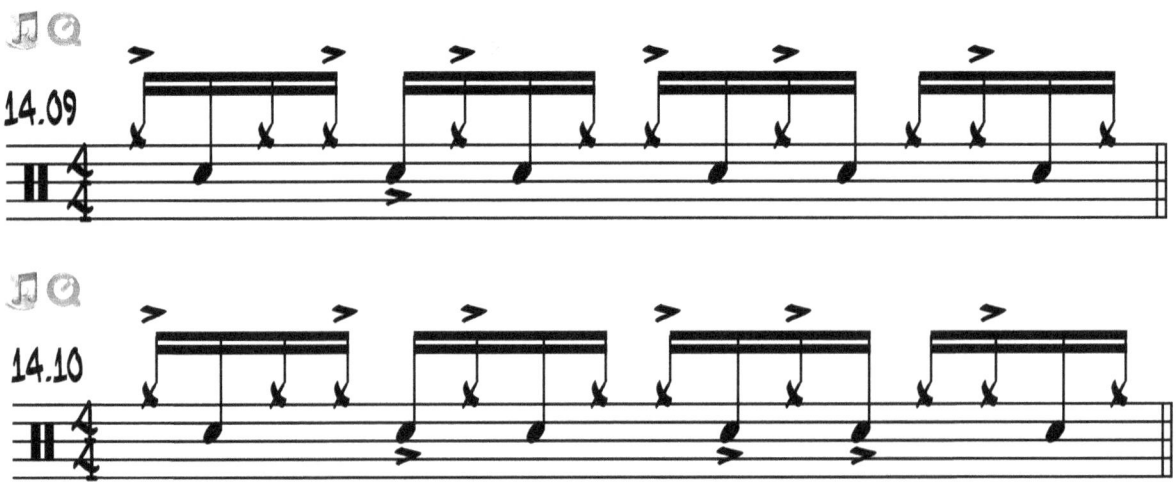

14.11 Here's a two-bar phrase with snare drum accents. Again, get this hand pattern down first before adding the bass drum.

The King Kong Beat

The King Kong beat that was mentioned in Section 8 is really a quasi-Latin rhythm that accents the "3" side of the 3-2 son clave. Here's another example using the fill-in technique, and adding the bass drum and a hi-hat opening to create a two-bar phrase.

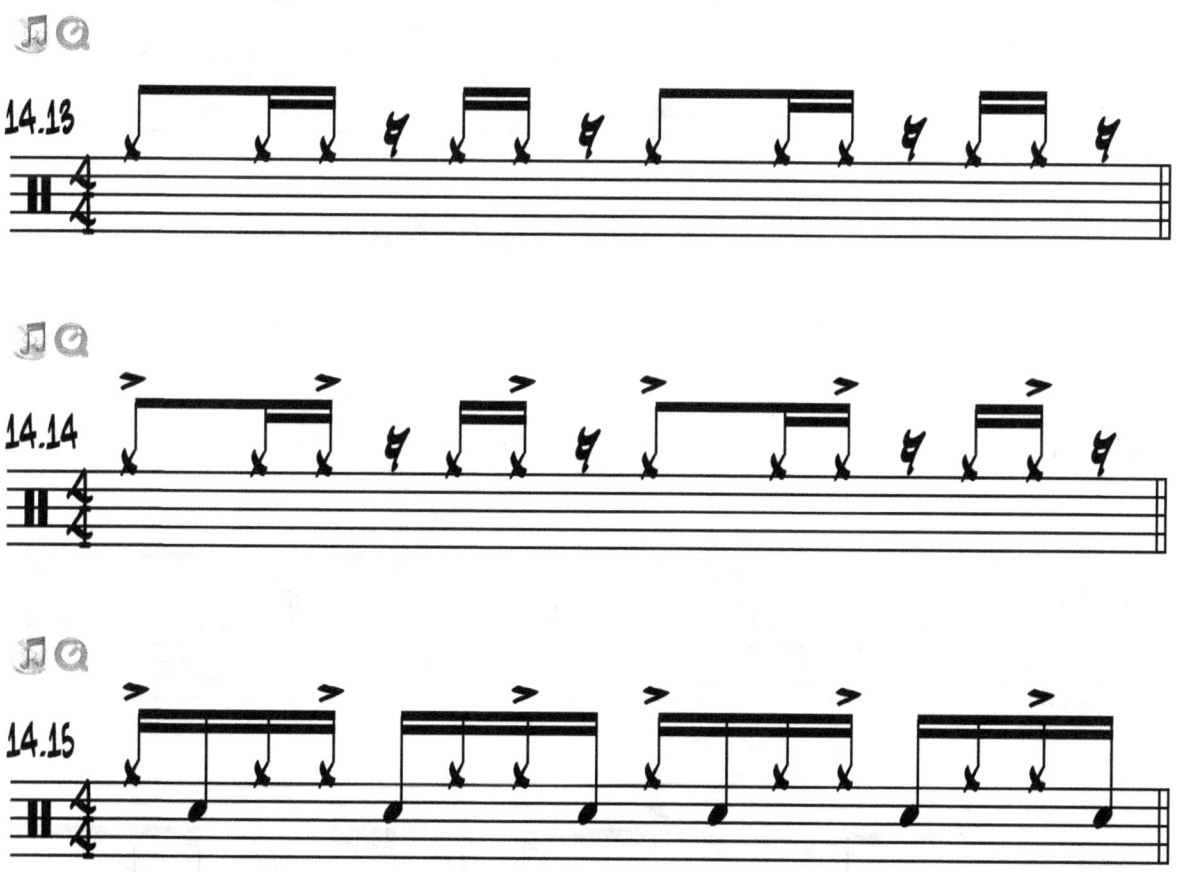

14.16

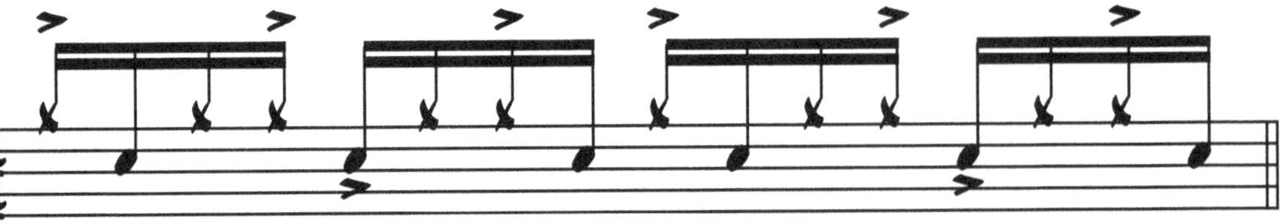

14.17

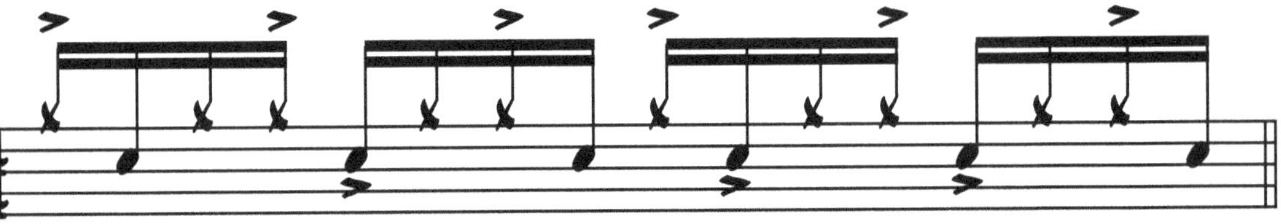

14.18

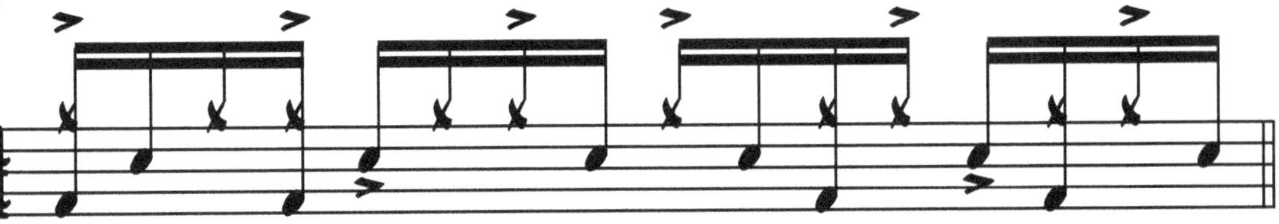

14.19A&8

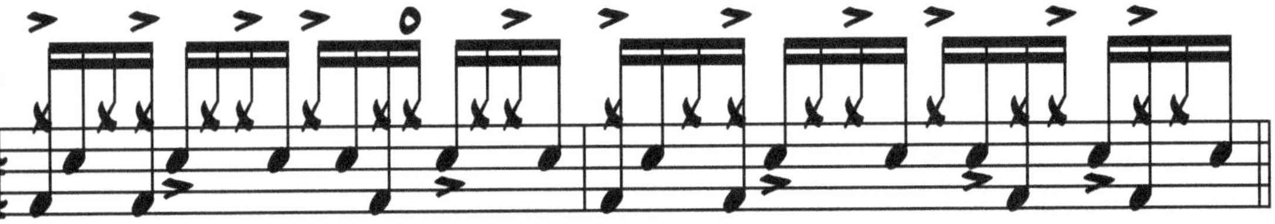

Another Latin-Style Right Hand Pattern

This is one of my favorite Latin-style right hand patterns. It has a group of three 16th notes (two notes and a rest) that cycle into "1" (see beat 14.05 A&B).

Apply the same fill-in idea, add the bass drum, and make a two-bar phrase.

14.20

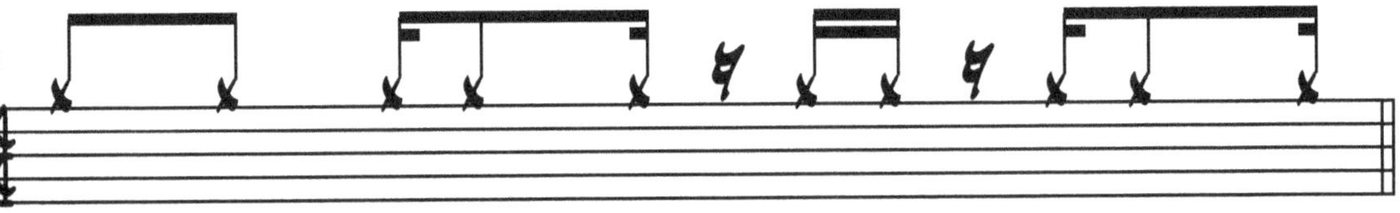

14.21

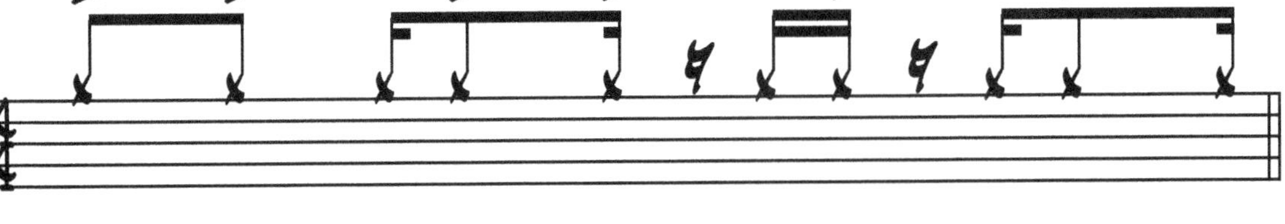

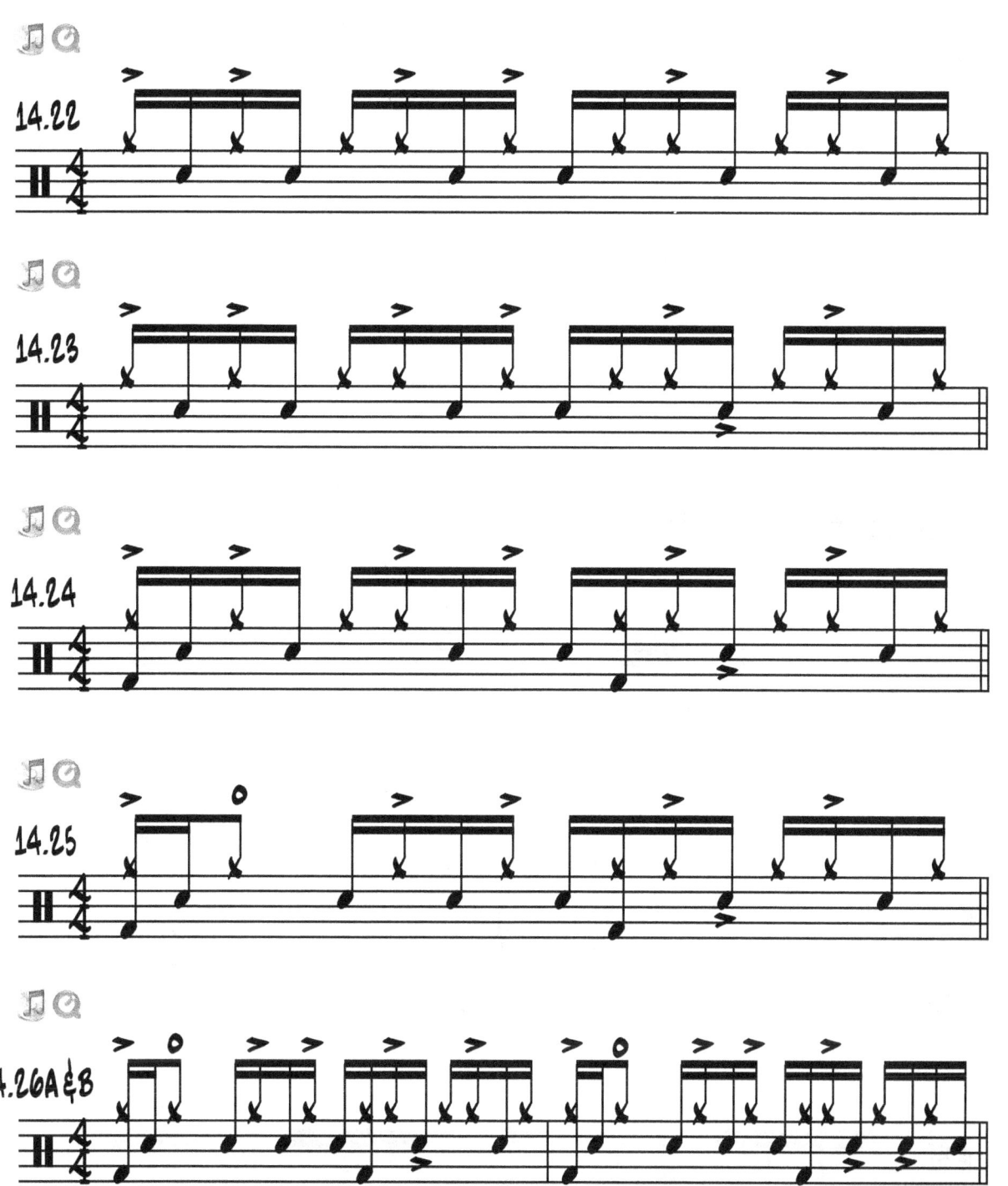

2-3 Latin Cascara

Use the same process with the 2-3 Latin cascara.

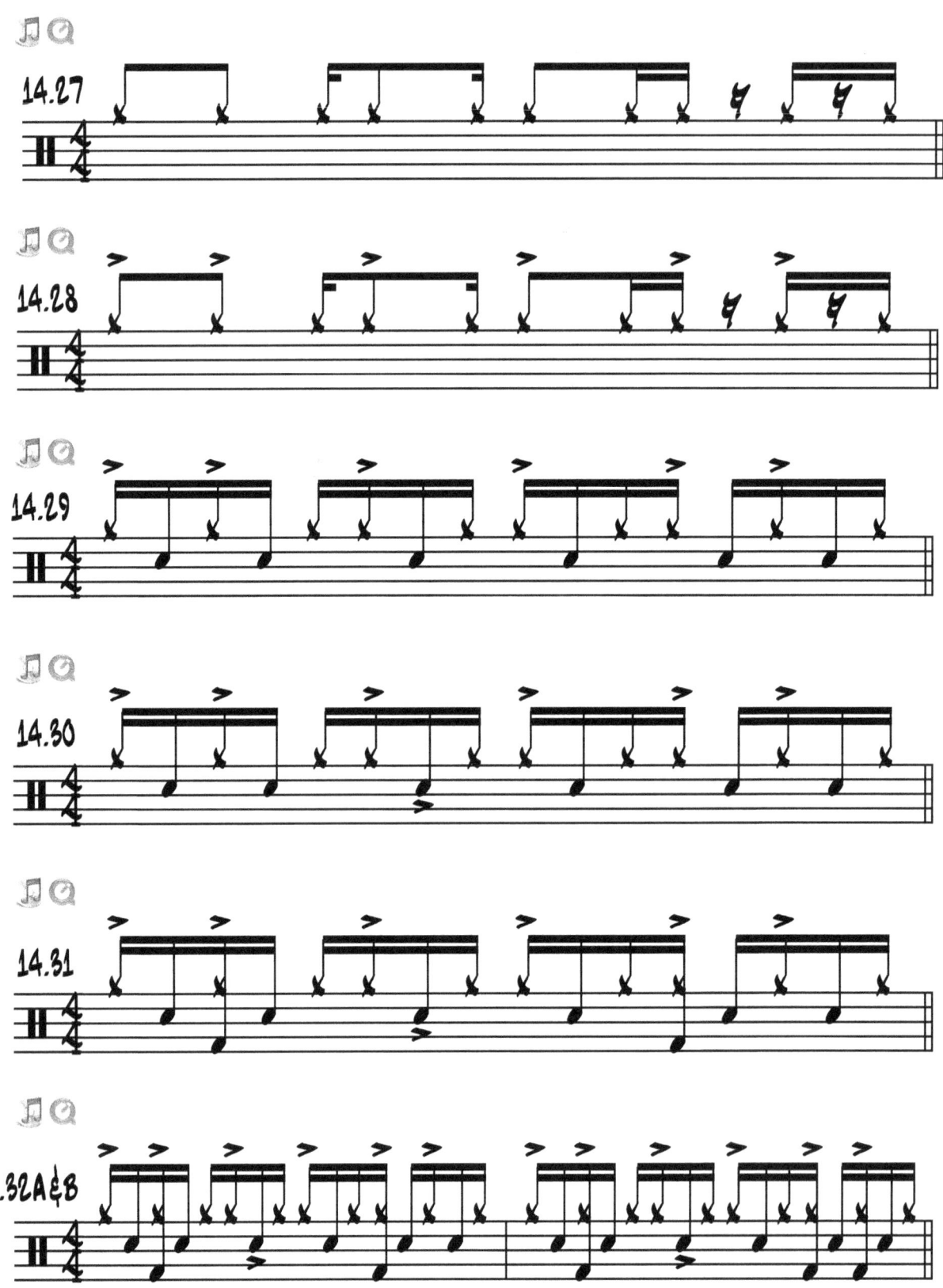

Greg FitzPatrick

ADVANCED FUNK DRUMMING 45

SECTION 15

Quarter-Note Hi-Hat Accents, Linear Style

15.01 This beat uses the single-stroke fill-in technique. It's comprised mainly of RLRL singles between the hi-hat and the snare drum using various accents.

15.03 The hi-hat is accented in quarter notes in this beat.

15.05 I used this beat on the song **"Peaches"** on my CD *Sensei*.

15.06 This is a mid-tempo swing-feel beat.

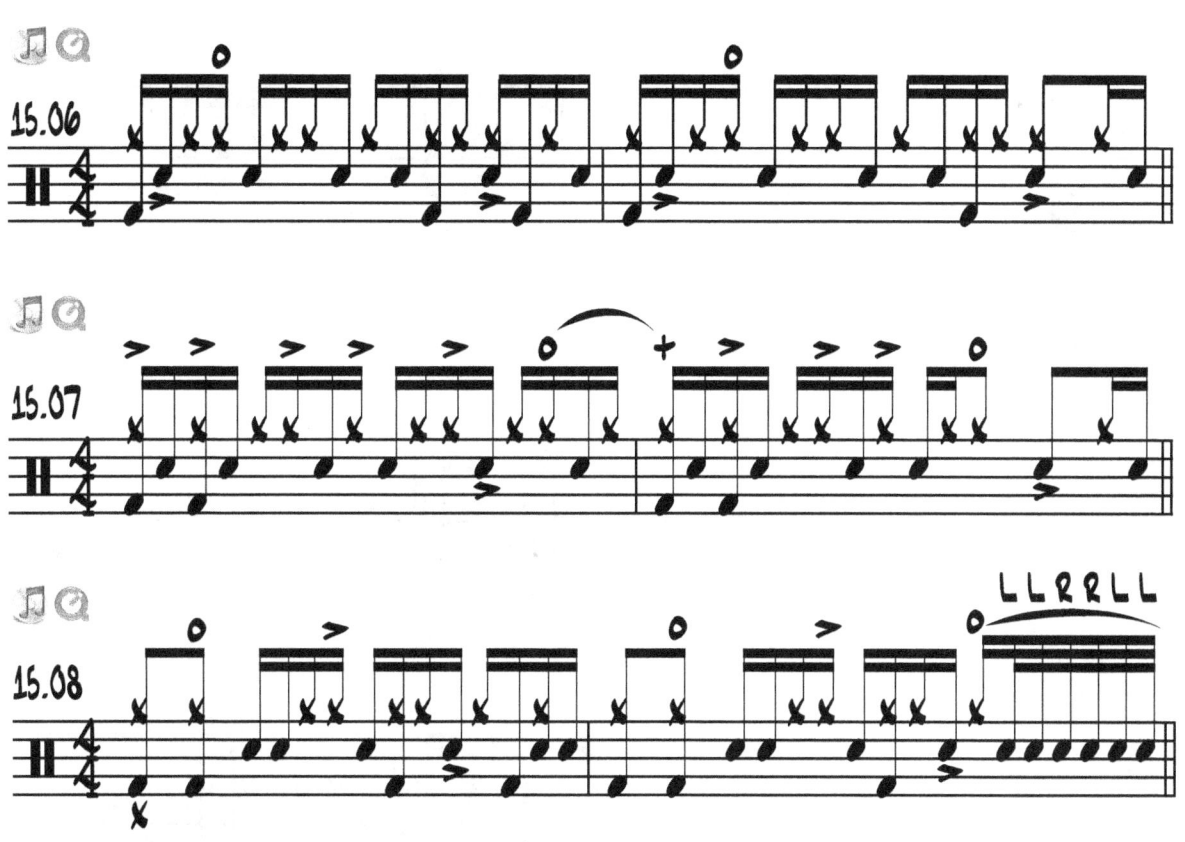

15.09 This beat incorporates a long buzz on "2" of the first bar.

15.10 This beat uses the single-stroke fill-in concept with quarter-note accents on the hi-hat.

15.11 Quarter notes on the hi-hat.

15.12 This is a slower, fat groove.

15.13 In this faster groove, the right hand comes off the hi-hat to play the snare drum on the "a of 4."

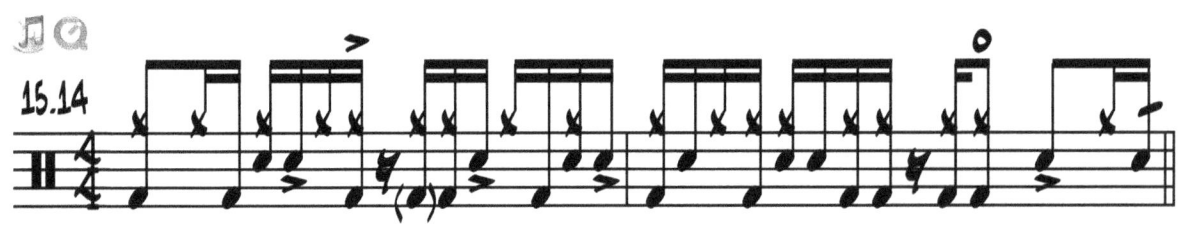

15.15 A&B A broken hi-hat pattern is the basis for this rhythm. I played a beat like this on the song **"Jabo"** on my CD *Energie*.

15.16 Here's a fast rhythm with the right hand playing a Latin pattern on the ride cymbal.

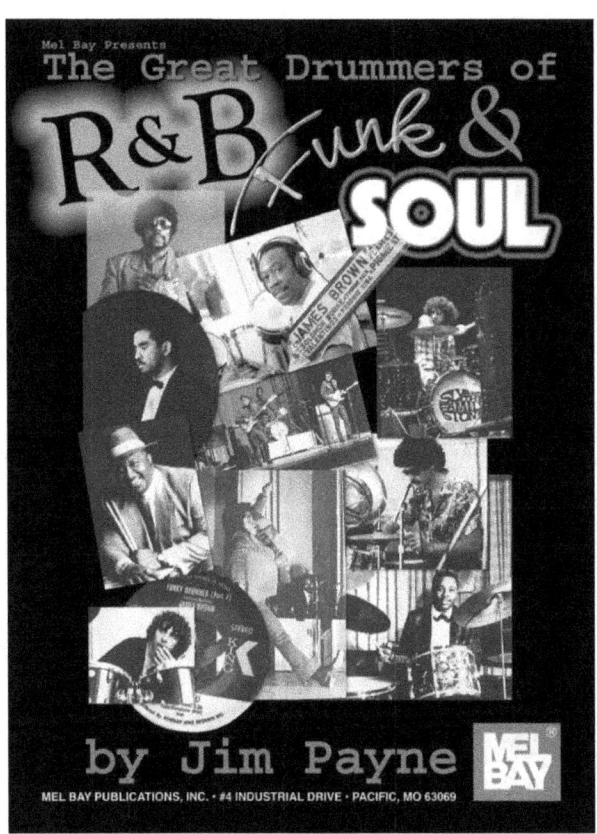
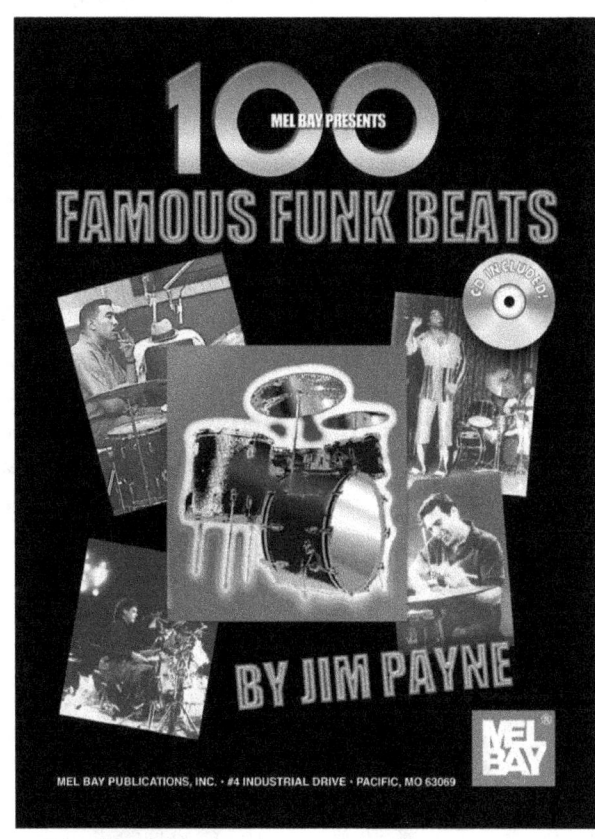

ADVANCED FUNK DRUMMING   49

These photos were taken by Patrick Barthe at a Jim Payne Band concert in Saou, France, in June 2008.

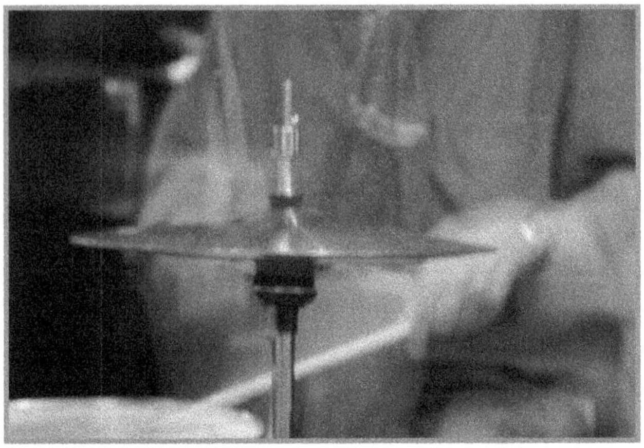

SECTION 16

No "1," Broken Hi-Hat Patterns, Swing Funk

Several of the beats in this section have no bass drum on "1." I call this **no "1."**

Although James Brown and George Clinton have talked a lot about "on the 1" and said a strong bass drum on the "1" has been a key element in a lot of their grooves, there is certainly no hard-and-fast rule. There's no reason why a groove can't be funky without the bass drum on "1." Latin and Afro-Cuban music is usually built around a strong rhythmic accent on "4," and the groove is super-powerful and just as funky.

16.01 No "1," with quarter-note accents on the hi-hat and no backbeat on "4" in the second bar.

16.02 The first bar has no bass drum on "1," but I played the bass drum on "1" the rest of the way. I added some improvisation at the end of each two-bar phrase.

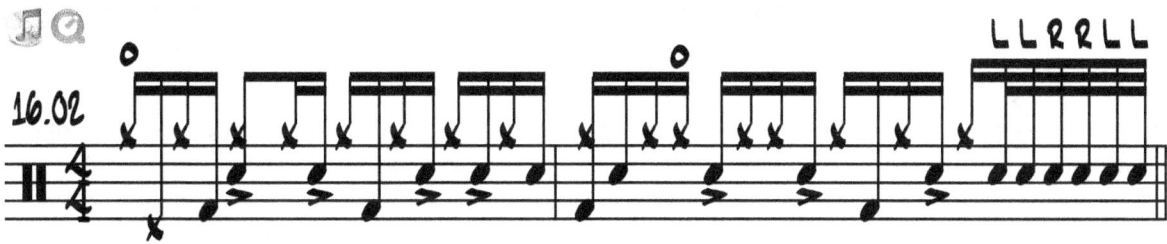

16.03 Medium swing funk.

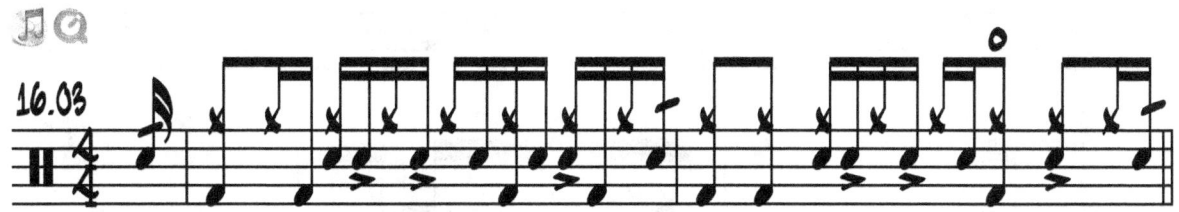

16.04 Fast and linear, with a hi-hat accent on "1."

16.05 Quarter-note accents on the hi-hat with a displaced backbeat in the second bar.

16.06 Medium-fast tempo, quarter-note accents on the hi-hat.

16.08 There's no "1" in this mostly linear four-bar phase. The right hand plays the snare on "4" of the fourth bar.

16.10 A&B Medium-slow tempo with a tom on the "&" and "a" of "2."

The view from the cabanon

Walking to work

SECTION 17

Triplet Grooves, Shuffles, Single-Stroke Fill-Ins

17.01 Here's a classic triplet groove.

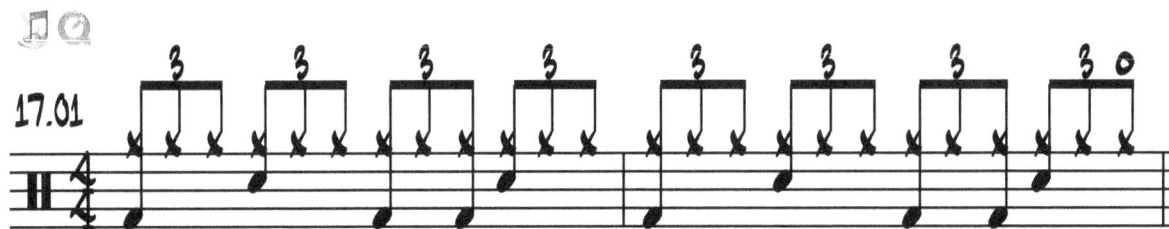

17.02 Here's a similar triplet groove with ghost notes added.

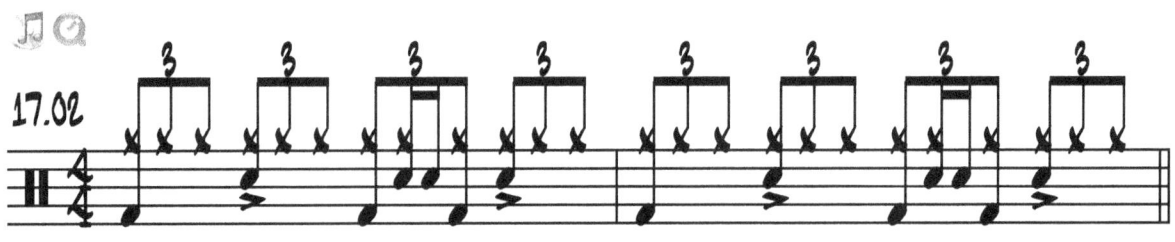

17.04 You can also play this triplet groove on the ride cymbal. The left foot plays each "let" on the hi-hat. (The "let" is the third note of a group of three 8th-note triplets.) This type of blues groove can be counted "1-trip-let, 2-trip-let, 3-trip-let, 4-trip-let."

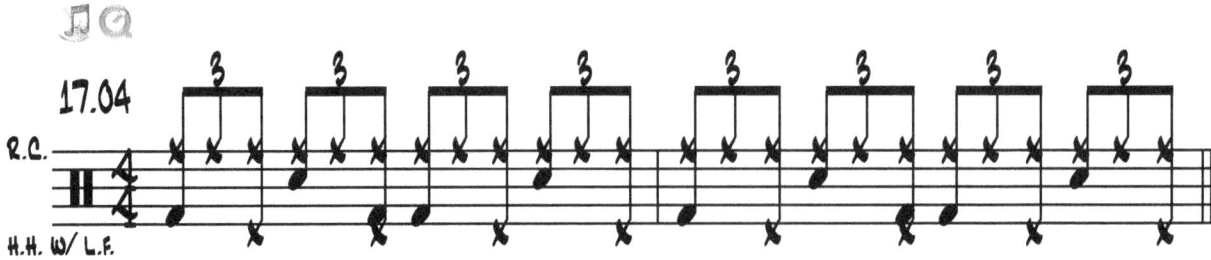

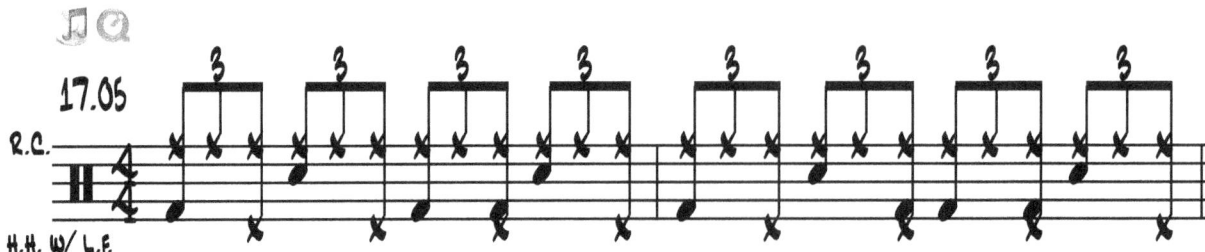

17.06 Triplet groove with ghost notes. The left foot plays every other triplet note on the hi-hat.

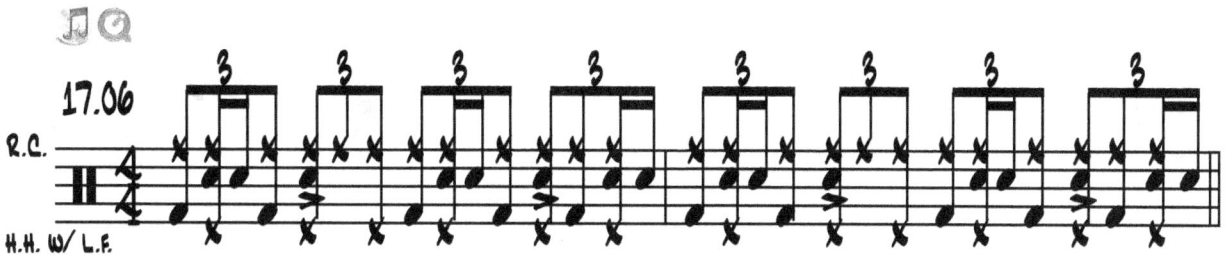

17.07 Shuffle triplet groove.

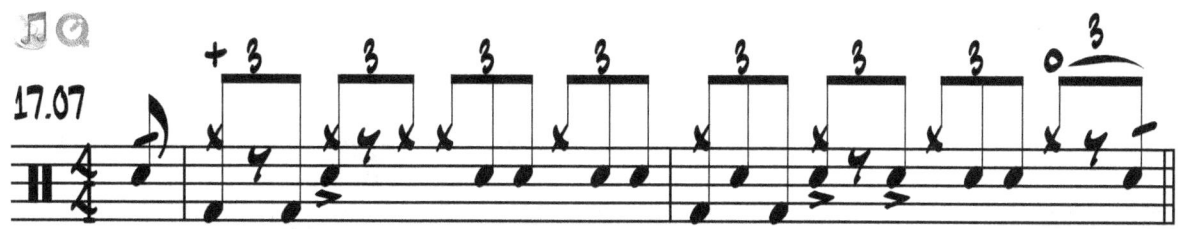

17.08 This half-time groove has a 6/8 Latin bell pattern on the ride cymbal. Use the fill-in technique with the left hand to play ghost notes, and then accent the backbeats on "3" of each bar. The right hand plays the floor tom on "4" of the fourth bar.

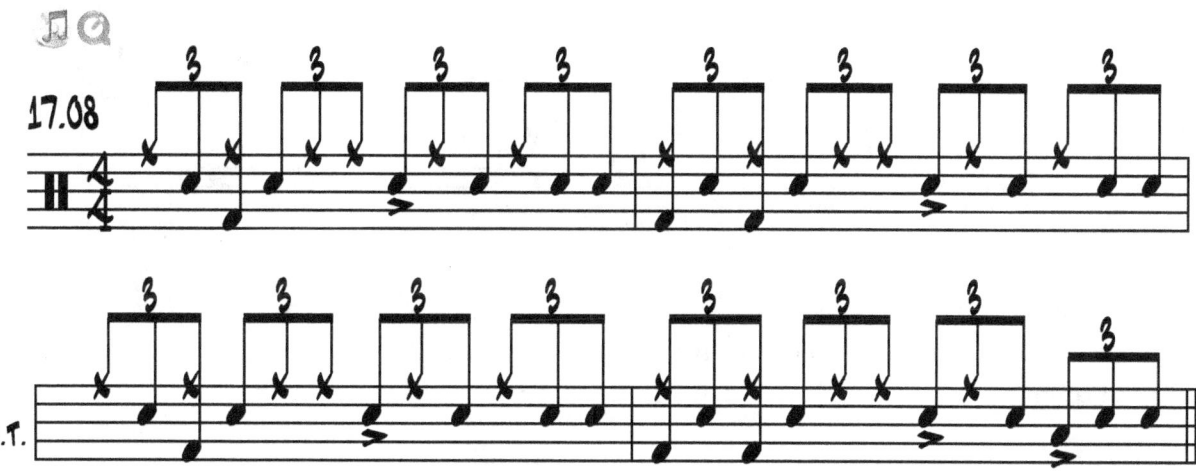

17.09 Four-bar, half-time triplet swing groove with a long hi-hat opening on "1."

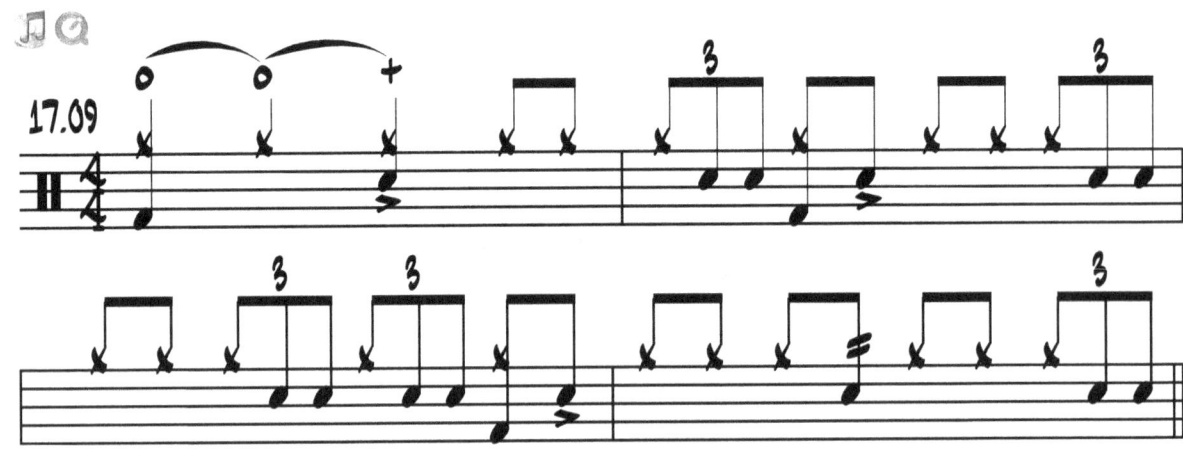

17.10 Up-tempo rhythm with quarter-note accents on the hi-hat and a displaced backbeat in the first bar.

17.11 Up-tempo rhythm with two figures taking up three quarter notes each (starting on "1") and two figures taking up one quarter note each ("3" and "4" of bar 2). The total, of course, is eight quarter notes, which equals two bars.

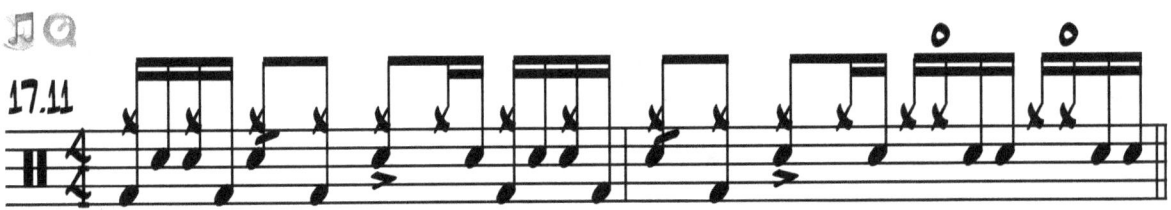

17.12 Medium-slow tempo, no "1" on the bass drum. The hi-hat is accented on the "1" of each bar. Use the single-stroke fill-in technique between the hi-hat and the snare drum. Ghost notes are added along with bass drum notes on the "a of 1" and the "e of 2."

17.13 A&B This beat is mostly linear, with no "1" on the bass drum and a broken hi-hat pattern.

SECTION 18

No "1," Groupings Of Three 16th Notes, Long Buzz

18.01 No "1" on the bass drum, mostly linear, with accented hi-hat. Somehow I put reverb on this beat in the video/audio files, and I can't get it off!

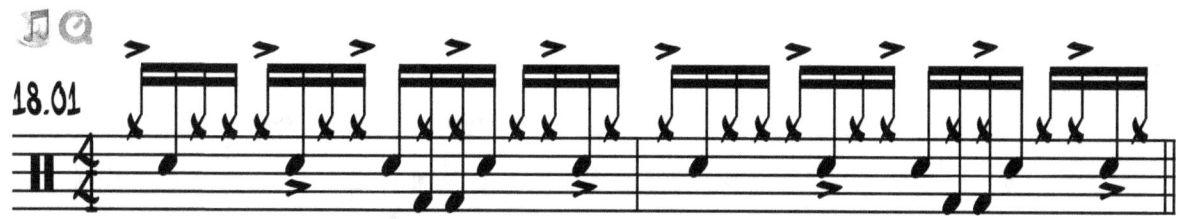

18.02 Medium-tempo, mostly linear rhythm with hi-hat accents.

18.05 Up-tempo rhythm using long buzzes and no "1" on the bass drum.

18.06 Medium up-tempo rhythm with a pattern of three 16th notes starting on the "1" of bar two.

18.07 Slow swing-funk groove.

18.08 Medium-tempo, softer funk groove.

18.09 Up-tempo linear groove with no "1" on the bass drum.

18.10 Up-tempo linear groove with no "1" on the bass drum.

ADVANCED FUNK DRUMMING

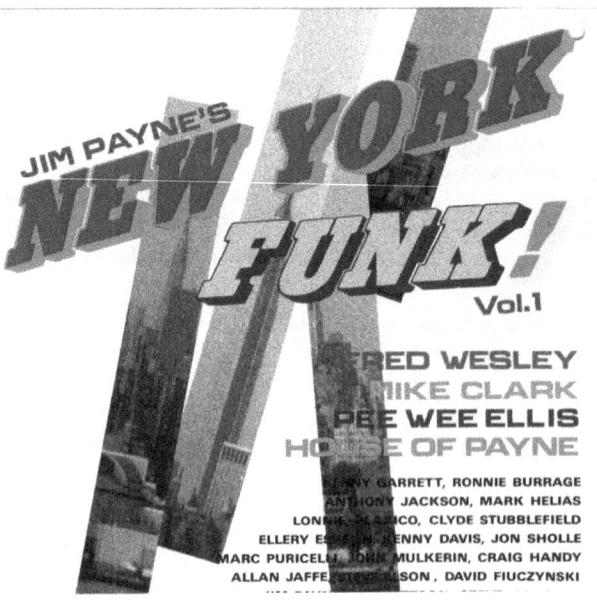
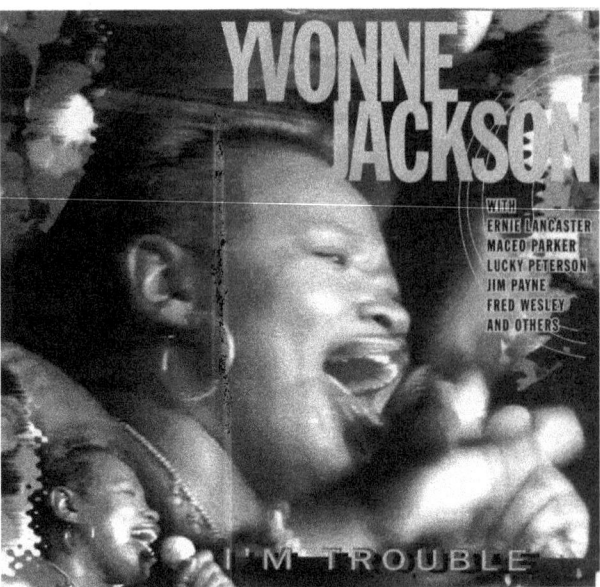

THE JIM PAYNE BAND

JIM PAYNE DRUMS   BILL BICKFORD GUITAR   JERRY Z HAMMOND ORGAN

JPAYNE@FUNKYDRUMMER.COM

L–R: Jerry Z, JP, Bill Bickford.

SECTION 19

Playing Over The "1," On The "1," Four-Bar Phrases

19.01 Four-bar phrase with a quarter-note hi-hat pattern.

19.02 Playing over the "1" and using the hi-hat/snare drum fill-in technique.

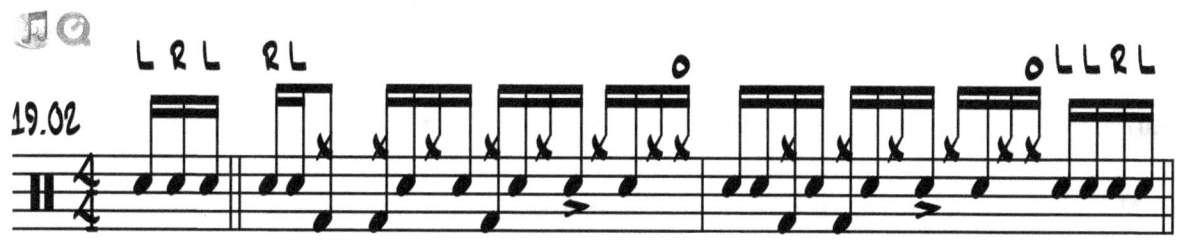

19.03 No "1" on the bass drum, with a hi-hat opening on the "e of 1."

19.04 Swing funk with a long hi-hat opening on "1." Notes in parentheses are played very softly.

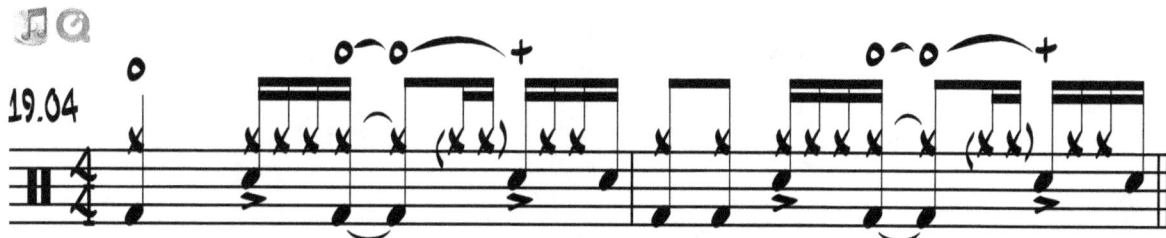

19.05 Mostly linear with no "1" on the bass drum.

19.06 Four-bar swing-funk rhythm with a stop.

19.07 A&B Funk groove with quarter notes on the hi-hat. The right hand comes off the hi-hat to play "4" on the snare drum in the first bar. (19.07A has a 16th-note ghost note on the snare drum on the "e of 1" in the second bar. I didn't play this note in 19.07B.)

19.08 Here's a four-bar linear funk rhythm.

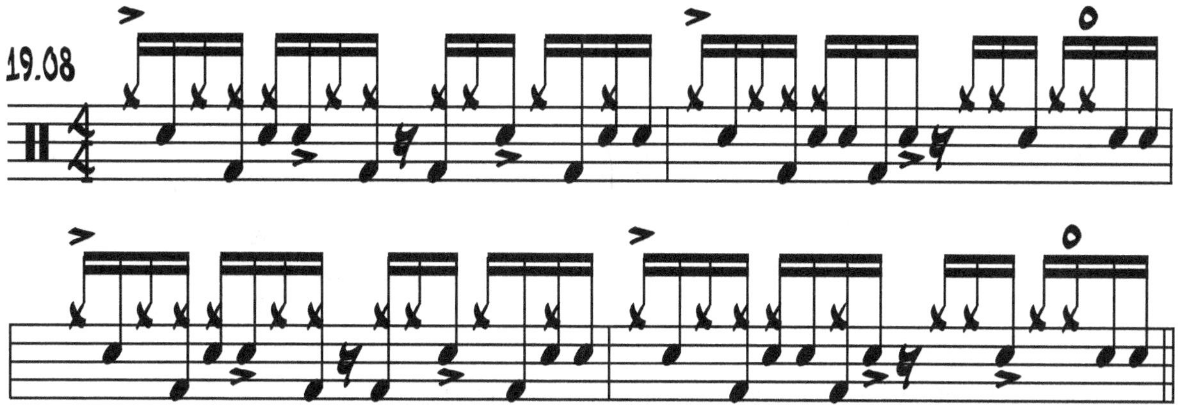

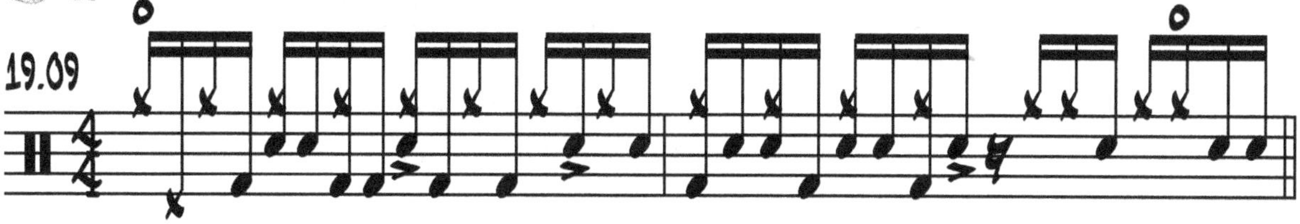

19.11 Medium up-tempo four-bar phrase with quarter-note accents on the hi-hat.

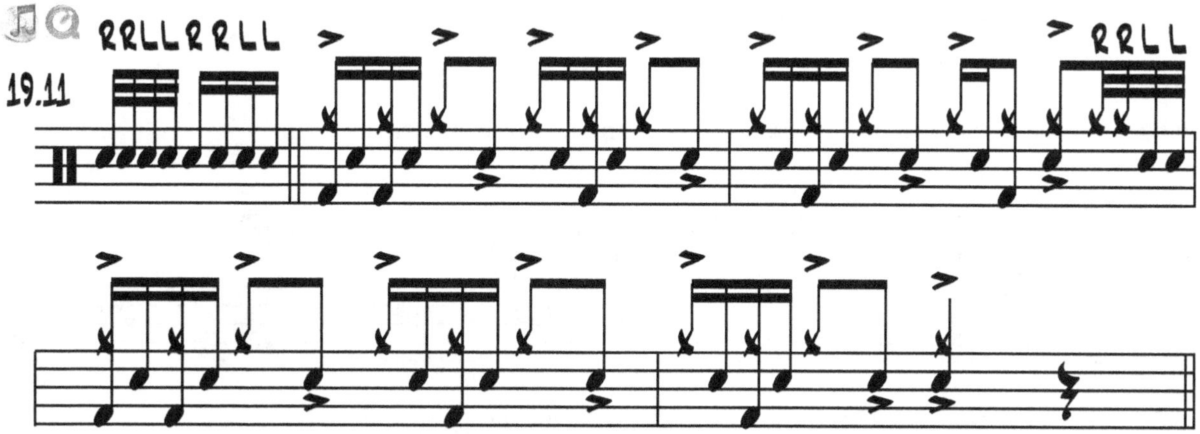

SECTION 20

Soft Dynamics, Grooves With Pickups, Long Hi-Hat Openings

20.01 Four-bar phrase.

20.02 Four-bar phrase. The hi-hat stays open on beat 4 and is struck very lightly so that the open sound continues until the "& of 4" (see the QuickTime clip). The "+" above the note indicates when to close the hi-hat with the left foot.

20.03 I used some variation when I repeated this rhythm in the QuickTime clip.

20.04 Four-bar phrase using buzz strokes and quarter-note accents on the hi-hat.

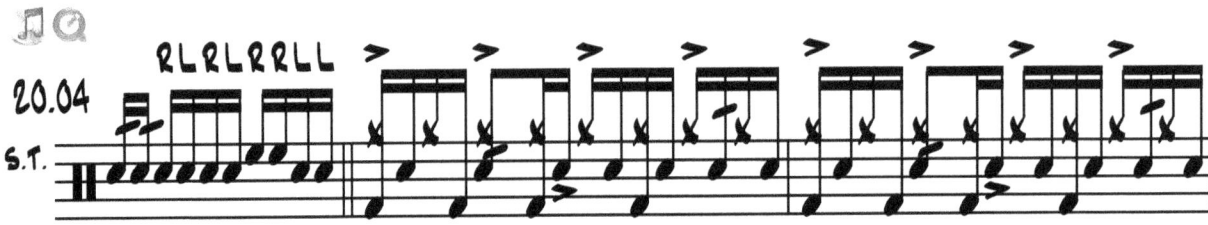

20.05A&B

20.06 Medium-tempo funk groove. No "1" on the bass drum.

20.06
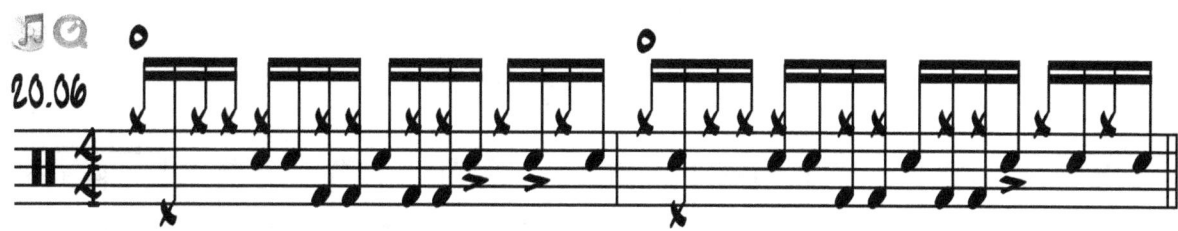

20.07 Four-bar New Orleans–style groove with a long hi-hat opening.

20.07

20.08 No "1" groove with the bass drum on the offbeats.

20.08

SECTION 21

More Hi-Hat Openings, Eight-Bar Groove, Use Of 32nd Notes

21.02 Up-tempo groove with the right hand playing quarter notes on the bell of the ride cymbal and the left foot playing the hi-hat on the "&" of every beat.

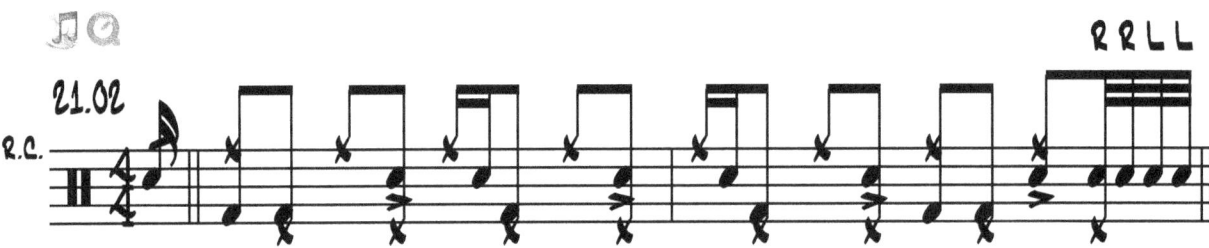

21.03 A&B Funk groove using half-open hi-hat notes.

21.04 Four-bar phrase.

21.05 "On the 1." Strong bass drum on "1" along with a long hi-hat opening.

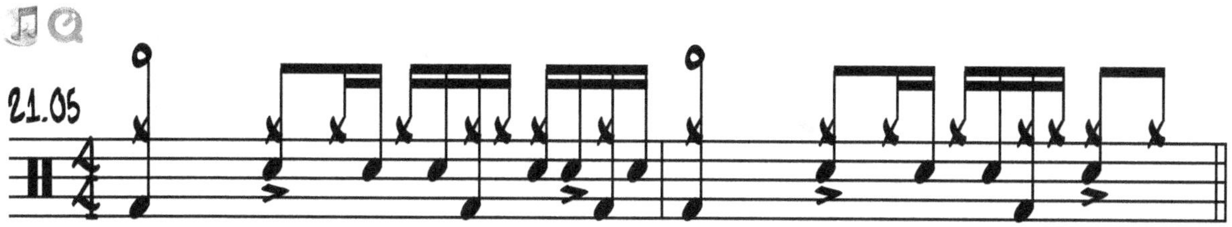

21.06 Four-bar phrases. The right hand comes off the hi-hat to play the snare on "1" of the fifth bar.

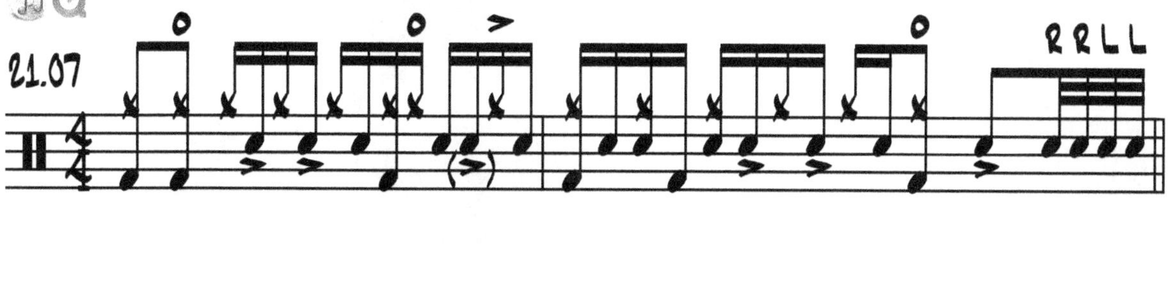

NOTES

www.ingramcontent.com/pod-product-compliance
Lightning Source LLC
Chambersburg PA
CBHW080349170426
43194CB00014B/2740